THE HIRING HANDBOOK

TIPS & TACTICS TO ATTRACT TOP TIER TALENT

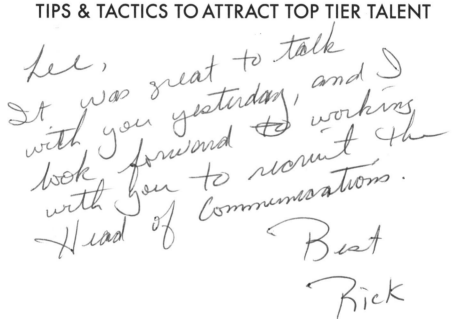

Lee,

It was great to talk with you yesterday, and I look forward to working with you to recruit the Head of Communications.

Best

Rick

Rick Linde

Table of Contents

I.	Introduction	1
II.	A Bit of Advice	3
III.	The Media/Technology Industry	5
IV.	Before Launching the Search	6
V.	Managing Expectations	13
VI.	Examining Internal Candidates	16
VII.	Your Options if You Don't Have a Strong Internal Candidate	19
VIII.	How to Choose a Search Firm	25
IX.	How to Manage the Search Firm	29
X.	Creating a Target List	35
XI.	Where Do Those Candidates Come From, Anyway?	37
XII.	Evaluating Resumes	40
XIII.	Diversity	45
XIV.	Phone Screens	51
XV.	Preparing for the Interview	52
XVI.	Different Interviews for Different Jobs	60
XVII.	Types of Interviews	64
XVIII.	Sample Questions	67
XIX.	The First Interview	70
XX.	Post-interview Assessment	86
XXI.	The Second Interview	91
XXII.	The Third Interview	95
XXIII.	Investigate the Finalist Candidate	97
XXIV.	Closing	103

XXV.	Onboarding	110
XXVI.	What If Your Search Fails?	111
XXVII.	Advice from the Experts	113

I. Introduction

As a senior executive, your success depends on the performance of your team. Hiring highly talented executives is therefore an essential part of your job. Yet you have received absolutely no relevant training, and you have no time to waste. This book contains all the steps necessary to hire a senior executive without screwing it up.

The Hiring Handbook focuses on the recruitment of senior managers and is intended to guide you through the process quickly and successfully. Although intended for the hiring manager, it can be useful for human resource executives, either to brush up on the subject or to educate the hiring manager. This book is brief, containing only the essential elements for interviewing and hiring. Although it could be more elaborate, I assume you have other things to do. You want to be good at interviewing, recognizing that anything less could easily result in an inferior hire, but this isn't something you want to study forever.

This handbook is organized in outline fashion for easy access. It is a resource guide to be kept on your office bookshelf and consulted when necessary. It is not intended to be read from cover to cover like a novel. Moreover, the information focuses on the tactical aspects of recruiting rather than lofty strategies, most of which are meaningless. We have all read too many leadership books that nobly proclaim that the secret to success is to hire only the best. As an experienced executive recruiter, I have never had a client who insisted on hiring the mediocre.

Most recruiting failures could be prevented by paying attention to the mechanics. Most of the mechanics involve regular communication and, like so many things, planning. By focusing on the recruitment of senior-level executives, more emphasis is placed on cultural fit rather than technical skills. This is not to say that technical skills are not important, but at a certain level they become almost taken for granted, whereas intangible issues assume greater importance.

II. **A Bit of Advice**

Most companies loudly proclaim that their employees are their most valuable assets. Then they behave as if quite the opposite were true, treating employees worse than they would treat their office furniture. Employee loyalty has disappeared largely because the company exhibits no loyalty whatsoever to the employee. Companies launch layoffs at the first whiff of a downturn. Employees, particularly your executives, are not commodities. No matter how automated business becomes, there will be a need for capable, creative decision makers. These people are in short supply, making it even more of a mystery as to why they are treated so shabbily.

If you, as a hiring manager, want to get the maximum value from your human capital, you need to get the best executives and then hang on to them. Your career will flourish and your company will thrive much more readily if you surround yourself with the best talent. While I am not an expert on talent retention, the obvious ways to hang on to your best people seem to be to treat them well and to resist the short-term fix of firing everybody whenever the quarterly numbers don't add up.

Acquiring the best talent is perhaps more complex. You will need some guidance to recruit the most capable executives. The best thing you can do is to develop a relationship with a trusted advisor or two. These advisors should understand the marketplace within your industry, have access to the right talent, and be unfailingly honest with you. They can also be good sounding boards for your own career path. A trusted advisor will be much more effective if you work with him/her repeatedly, allowing him/her to understand how decisions are made, the personalities of the people making them, and the chemistry of the organization. If you work for very large company, sometimes those trusted advisors may be a part of an internal recruitment team. Sometimes that works. What doesn't work over the long haul is cutting corners.

Another thing that doesn't work is for you to delegate the work and remove yourself from the process. To get the right person in the right position, you are going to have to remain engaged. While your human resources department certainly should be involved, you will need to stay close to the recruiting process, converse regularly with the recruiter, assess prospective candidates, and make decisions. Otherwise you will not win the arms race for talent.

III. The Media/Technology Industry

I lead an executive search boutique focused on senior-level recruiting in the digital media space, the intersection between technology and media and between content and commerce. This is an exciting time to be working in this arena. The ways people communicate and consume information seem to be changing on a monthly basis. Not everyone is filled with optimism, however. The old ways of making money are threatened, and it is far from clear what the new ways will be. It is nevertheless an exciting time. When asked to advise young people about future career opportunities, I invariably and enthusiastically recommend media and technology. While other industries undoubtedly possess promise, it would be hard to find another that compares.

Now that you have some background on the purpose and scope of the *Hiring Handbook*, I hope it proves useful.

IV. **Before Launching the Search**

a. DEFINE THE JOB: Always begin your recruiting efforts by defining the role via a thorough job description. Since it is easier to edit a job description than to write one from scratch, ask human resources for the present job description. If one is not available, perhaps you can unearth one from a similar position to use as a template. Don't blindly accept whatever is set down on paper, however. Look to see if the job has changed. Think about the incumbent, if there is one, to see what characteristics you would like to retain and which ones you would like to avoid. Look at your department to identify unmet needs. Can these be incorporated into this position? Or perhaps this vacancy may trigger a reallocation of responsibilities throughout your team. Be honest; does this job even need to be filled? Create a job description that addresses your specific needs:

    i. Write a job description that includes:

        1. Company background

        2. Educational requirements

        3. Key responsibilities

        4. Necessary experiences

5. Key deliverables

6. Skills, attitudes, and behaviors

7. Reporting relationships, both up and down. Be clear about where the position reports and what staff and resources will be assigned.

8. Don't specify compensation, as this will be a document available to all prying eyes, including internal ones.

9. Avoid jargon and clichés.

ii. Define the value the successful candidate will provide. What is the successful candidate expected to accomplish? Identify what metrics will be used to determine success. When launching a new search, my favorite question to the client is, "What do you expect the successful candidate to accomplish in year one?" Successful recruiting is front-end loaded. If you are careful to determine what you really need, you are much more likely to find it.

iii. Whenever possible, use action words (e.g., "increase sales by 11%").

iv. Make sure the title and job grade are appropriate for the actual responsibilities of the job. It is remarkable how often a description of qualifications will be outrageously inflated beyond the actual level of the job.

v. If possible, show your draft version of the job description to the incumbent to see if he/she has suggestions.

vi. Build consensus from the stakeholders, including your boss, peers, HR, and perhaps even key reports. Get them in a room to identify the key challenges and responsibilities, incorporating this information into the job description. Focus on the value this person will bring, what you want the successful candidate to accomplish. Get everyone's input and write it all down. Hammer out disagreements, but be realistic. Many such job descriptions require candidates to walk on water. That is unrealistic and will hinder your chances of success. When you are finished, distribute the memo. Gaining consensus now will prevent different agendas from emerging down the road. Later, if a key stakeholder starts to trumpet some new agenda, you can wave this document in front of him/her to remain on track..

b. DETERMINE COMPENSATION:

i. If you work in a large, established company, decisions on compensation may have already been made.

ii. In small companies, or for new positions within large ones, there is greater flexibility. For advice, talk with an executive recruiter, a compensation consultant, or a peer in a similar organization. Because this is how they earn their living, compensation consultants typically will urge you to do a market study. This is probably unnecessary unless you are creating a whole new category of positions or if you had chronic trouble in hiring.

iii. A dose of reality: Don't adopt compensation parameters at the market average and expect candidates at the ninety-ninth percentile.

iv. Flexibility: Breaching salary limits may be necessary if trying to attract a star.

v. Bonus: Nearly all positions above a base salary of $200,000 offer a targeted bonus exceeding 15 percent of salary, often much higher, especially for more senior roles. The bonus is usually paid annually and is based on achieving a combination of company and personal goals. Bonus targets vary widely, depending on industry, company, and functional responsibilities. Senior-level sales management positions, for example, often feature bonuses of 100 percent of base salary. Performance targets should be aggressive but reasonable, since executives usually consider the bonus part of their anticipated compensation, assuming good performance (assuming bad performance, they probably won't have a job). While this represents the norm in the marketplace, there are countless examples of companies that pay less of a bonus or none at all, particularly if company performance has suffered in the prior year.

vi. Equity/long-term incentive: Companies have a dizzying array of long-term programs designed to encourage capable employees to remain with the organization and to work hard to increase its long-term value. Most of the time companies' participation is fixed, so there is no point negotiating for more shares, options, RSUs, whatever the program offers. Sometimes, especially with smaller or privately held companies, the equity package may vary depending on how well the incoming executive negotiates.

c. EVALUATE YOUR ORGANIZATION: An efficient, sensible organizational structure is critical to success. If, for example, you intend to recruit someone to compensate for an awkward organizational structure or to work around a poor performer, tackle the real problem. Reorganize. In addition, don't create a job with more than seven or eight direct reports and make sure everyone's role is clearly defined.

d. CONSIDER THE CULTURAL FIT: Clients often (consciously or unconsciously) seek out candidates who possess similar educational credentials and backgrounds. There are plusses to this approach. As the boss, you may relate better to the candidate. Ask yourself if that is really what is needed, however. Perhaps you need a different set of skills or a different way of looking at things to complement your own. Perhaps you need diversity.

    i. First, it is important to understand your own company culture. Take a look at the sort of people who succeed; try to identify characteristics those people possess.

    ii. If you are the hiring manager, talk to HR to see if they have any insight.

    iii. Don't waste time writing or reviewing corporate mission statements that feature nonsense about "being the best." Most of that is so embarrassing. It may instill pride among those who already belong to the organization, but it offers little help in identifying genuine cultural attributes. These lofty sentiments may depict the company as its leaders would like it to be, but it probably is not grounded in reality.

    iv. In examining the culture of your company, it helps to make some comparisons against other organizations you are familiar with. It also helps to identify the characteristics you are looking to avoid, as well as those you want to attract. Once you have developed a few attributes, test them with coworkers to see how they might clarify your description.

e. **RELOCATION:** Moving someone from out of town is expensive. Whether you need to go to this extra trouble will largely be a function of your geography. In a large metropolitan area or a hotbed of a particular industry, you will likely be able to focus your search locally. Even if you are willing to foot the bill, it has become increasingly difficult to entice people to move. Family considerations are often to blame, with the increase of two-income families, the need to care for aging parents, and a desire not to interrupt children's education as the primary deterrents. Companies in smaller or remote locations suffer as a result. In these instances, you should initially focus on local candidates and expand geographic boundaries later if the talent just isn't available. Make sure you have the budget for it. If the candidate owns his/her home, it could easily cost you $100,000 to move someone. While companies no longer purchase real estate or take out mortgages anymore, relocation is still a big ticket item and a headache.

f. SHORT VERSUS LONG-TERM CONSIDERATIONS: Most of the time you will be looking for a candidate who will remain and grow in the company for years. On the other hand, you occasionally might need an employee to fix an urgent problem. Be honest. It is important to recognize what sort of situation you are in. For example, if you are concerned primarily with fixing a short-term emergency, then a history of job hopping becomes less of a deterrent. If you do want a long-term employee, ask some probing questions:

   i. How will your boss react when you resign?

   ii. What are the most frustrating aspects of your current job?

   iii. How did your boss contribute to your desire to leave the company?

   iv. What did you learn from changing jobs?

   v. Describe the best company you have worked for and tell me what you liked about it.

   vi. Why were you let go? (This is a very useful question that can potentially be double checked through a reference at the company.)

V. **Managing Expectations**

a. THE PERFECT CANDIDATE: Start with the understanding that no candidate is perfect. Identify the key criteria for success and compare each candidate against those items. Don't get sidetracked by looking for perfection. Too often clients will jettison a candidate if they discover a minor flaw. That's a mistake unless the shortcoming would prevent the person from doing a good job. Holding out for perfection is a waste of time and money.

b. LATERAL MOVES VERSUS A STEP UP: Decide whether you are looking for a candidate who has already performed all the job requirements. On the surface, it appears obvious that you should prefer candidates who have already covered all the bases. Yes, such a candidate will be able to handle all aspects of the job immediately, but you have to wonder about a candidate willing to accept a lateral move, even if you are willing to pay a few more dollars. Hiring someone who is too senior for the job can be expensive. Moreover, that person may not stick around if the job is not challenging. Will the successful candidate jump ship when the economy picks up and another more senior job comes along? Then you have to start the search process all over again. I recommend the other scenario. Hire candidates for whom the job represents a step up in their career. This is also the way to attract the brightest and most talented with the best long-term potential.

c. LONG-TERM GOALS: These days, so many recruitments are designed to fix a specific, immediate, urgent problem. Little thought is given to a long-term career path. Do you want to hire someone who can stick a finger in the dike to stop a leak or someone who will become a future leader of the company? If feasible, the second alternative is obviously preferable to you, your company, and the candidate. Thinking this way forces you to think more about the candidates' overall talent and less about whether they possess the particular skills to fix a specific problem.

d. CHANGE AGENTS: Be wary if your recruiting plans call for recruiting a change agent (*don't you just hate that phrase?*) to make significant improvements in the way your organization does business. That usually doesn't work. Organizational change has to flow from the top. It is just unfair to put someone in at the middle of the hierarchy and expect that person to alter the entire organization in a positive way. Even putting someone new in at the top often doesn't work if you are looking for a structural shift, particularly if yours is a large company. Outsiders don't have relationships and credibility within the organization. Many so-called change agents have very sharp elbows too, making it even less likely that people will follow their plans. Most likely there will be an organ rejection. This is not to say that companies cannot make real changes, but the change has to be enthusiastically, energetically endorsed right from the top. The person leading the transition needs to have the credibility and leadership to get the rest of the team to follow.

e. TIMING: Plan ahead. Hiring a senior-level executive usually requires ninety days. Midlevel hires are perhaps less, largely because you are likely to be less picky. For senior-level hires, it will take four to five weeks just to see good candidates. This can be shortened if your recruiter has worked extensively in the field. After the candidates are presented, you will need to interview them, which takes at least a couple of weeks, more if you or your team gets busy and needs to postpone meetings. You also need to allow time for checking references, courting the finalist candidate, negotiating compensation, and any delays that occur unexpectedly. It is difficult to shorten this timeline. The biggest source of delays is often the client him/herself. Much of it is spent waiting for the hiring manager and the team to interview candidates and respond with feedback. At the front end of the search, many clients proclaim that this recruitment is the most important thing on their agenda. Then interruptions and emergencies occur. A small subset of clients refuses to allow distractions to interfere, perhaps because they are less busy, or more organized, or have truly made the recruitment a priority. This group is able to get the search done quickly. Recommendation: either make up your mind at the outset of the search to refuse to get distracted or adjust your expectations accordingly.

VI. **Examining Internal Candidates**

a. Look at your bench: The best way to fill an opening is to have a strong cadre of internal candidates who have been groomed and are ready for promotion. Recruiting outsiders is useful only if this process has broken down or if you need new blood and new ideas.

b. Be objective: When evaluating internal candidates, do so in the same dispassionate way you would examine an external one: compare this person's experiences against the job description. This allows you to push political considerations off the table.

c. Caution: While internal candidates may be loyal and successful, they are probably performing a different job and may not be suitable for yours. Resist the pressure to accept an unacceptable candidate simply to reward a loyal but marginal or inappropriate player.

d. Keep communicating: During the recruitment process, internal candidates are often left in the dark about their chances for the promotion. This can be terribly demoralizing, especially if the process drags on. Mishandling the expectations of internal candidates will be perceived as a betrayal. Honest and frequent communication is essential or the disappointed employee will begin looking for employment elsewhere. By communicating thoughtfully, you will likely be able to keep that person motivated even if he/she doesn't get the promotion.

e. So-so candidates: Sometimes a promising but not exceptional internal candidate will surface. You, the hiring manager, may find yourself in "like" but not in "love". This leaves you wondering if you should promote the person or launch an external search. One interesting solution is to authorize an external search, but only for a month. This will be long enough for a good recruiter to scour the marketplace and identify a slate of capable candidates. In this month you, the hiring manager, will likely see resumes, but you probably won't have time to interview the individuals behind them. However, by looking at these resumes, you should be able to determine whether to hire the internal candidate or continue the search. If the internal person is as good as or better than those identified externally, promote that person and cancel the search. In exchange for a modest fee (one month's retainer), you now have the confidence of having made the right choice. If the external candidates are superior, as they often are, you should be prepared to continue the search and have an unpleasant conversation with the aspiring internal candidate.

f. Honesty: Dealing with internal candidates is delicate, since they are eager for promotion and may already be looking on the outside. Failure to get the job could drive them out of the company. But fear of losing a respected employee should not hold you hostage in making a hiring decision. If the internal candidate is not qualified for the new role, regular feedback is essential to prevent hard feelings. Perhaps that employee should move on to greener pastures if the right growth opportunities do not exist at your company. A candid discussion of the candidate's anticipated career progression is essential.

VII. **Your Options if You Don't Have a Strong Internal Candidate**

a. RETAINED SEARCH: A search firm gets paid a retainer as the search unfolds and is usually hired for positions where total cash compensation exceeds $175,000. The retained recruiter makes a commitment to continue to work on your recruitment until it is completed successfully. The recruiter therefore makes the most money when the search is completed quickly, not when it drags on. In a retained search, the retainer is based on one-third of the projected cash compensation required to attract the successful candidate. This will include the anticipated base salary and the targeted annual bonus. Most recruiters will use a conservative estimate of compensation so that there is no chance that the retainer will be less than a third of the first year's total pay. Some clients complain that the bonus offered to the successful candidate is not guaranteed and should not be included in fee considerations. The customary practice, however, is to include the estimated first year's bonus in the fee calculations. By negotiating, you may reduce the fee to 30 percent of the total package. You may even be able to get the recruiter to accept less, depending on the recruiter's workload, the size of the fee, the anticipated future volume of business from your company, etc. Some recruiters charge for a portion of the equity to be offered to the successful candidate, but this is uncommon. When it occurs at all, it usually involves searches with small, venture-backed companies where cash compensation may be below market rates but the potential value of the equity makes up for it. Retained recruiters also charge for expenses, either actual expenses incurred in the course of the search or a prorated percentage of the fee.

b. CONTINGENCY RECRUITMENT: These firms are paid only upon completion of the search. They usually operate at lower levels than retained recruiters, although some work on quite senior jobs, particularly in the financial services and legal industries. Contingency firms tend to be niche players who are well versed in a specific industry or function. Taking them away from their comfort zone is a waste of time. On the surface, contingency recruiters are appealing since you incur no up-front commitment, but the sad truth is that they cannot afford to spend much time on your problem because they are not being paid to do so. Many will not meet candidates before introducing them, and even more will simply disgorge the contents of their databases, hoping you like some of the resumes they send. If you feel that you are being neglected during a contingency recruitment, you probably are. The headhunter has probably moved on to more promising assignments, having concluded that yours is unlikely to yield a fee. It is perfectly legitimate to authorize several contingency firms to work on the same assignment. In this case, make sure to establish rules as to who "owns" a candidate once that person has been introduced. Failure to do this could result in paying two fees if two firms introduce the same person. Don't let a contingency recruitment drag on. If the recruiter has decent candidates, you will know within a few weeks. The fees charged by contingency recruiters are in the neighborhood of 20–25 percent of the base salary, decidedly less than those charged by retained firms. Contingency recruiting is a notoriously precarious way to earn a living. Every contingency headhunter has had many unfortunate experiences of getting all the way to the finish line of a search only to have the client decide not to complete the search or hire someone from another firm. Hence many good contingency recruiters try to charge retainers to achieve greater financial stability.

c. CONTAINER: (a word play on CONtingency and reTAINER, get it?) This involves elements of both. An up-front commitment is paid to the firm, but no further payment is required until completion of the search. This model is growing in popularity, particularly among contingency firms that want to gain a foothold in the retained market. In some cases the financial commitment can be nominal, just enough to reassure the recruiter that you are dealing only with him/her. In others the recruiter may charge two monthly retainers but agree to waive the final one until the successful conclusion of the search. If the search is not completed, you will not owe the final payment.

d. RESEARCH FIRMS: These are usually small firms or individuals working from home who provide lists of names, titles, and phone numbers for you to call from target companies you have defined. Sometimes they will develop candidates for you too, making the initial calls, inquiring about the candidate's interest, and doing some preliminary screening. Their fees are earned on an hourly basis. Most of them also provide this service to search firms, who subcontract the initial calling efforts. Most research firms are not prepared to interview candidates or bring the process to conclusion. Much of the heavy lifting is left to you. Although cheap, this should not be your first choice unless you are really prepared to do the search yourself.

e. DOING IT YOURSELF:

i. Hiring a permanent staff of internal recruiters. Sometimes internal recruiters are expected to hire outside recruiters and manage the search process, sometimes they do the recruiting themselves. Often they do a combination of both, depending on the volume of work. Many large organizations that have a significant search volume have experimented with hiring a permanent staff of recruiters who handle all the staffing needs of the company. This potentially offers a powerful cost savings when compared with paying search fees. However, these savings depend on hiring cheap people, since the whole point of the exercise is to save money. However, this often does not work. Like most things, executive recruiting requires talented, experienced practitioners. They tend to be expensive. If you hire a talented (expensive) internal staff, pretty soon the cost difference between paying the internal team and outsourcing the work disappears. If your recruiting volume subsides, you will also find yourself paying for a recruiting staff that isn't doing any recruiting. This is an expensive fixed cost. Nevertheless, some companies successfully maintain a staff of permanent internal recruiters who provide good service to their companies.

ii. Hiring freelance contract recruiters on an ad hoc basis. This can be very effective and inexpensive, since you are not saddled with a fixed expense after the hiring crush subsides. It tends to work only for lower- and mid-level hiring, however. The people available to do this sort of work often are not equipped to interact effectively on senior-level assignments.

iii. Employee referral programs. Usually a stipend is awarded to the employee for a successful referral. This sort of networking can be the most efficient way of finding great employees. The stipends are often minimal, certainly less than search fees, and these candidates often remain with your company longest. There are tales of employees neglecting their jobs to earn referral fees, so be alert that your referral program does not create a host of new problems. On the other hand, constant reminding is necessary to prevent employees from forgetting about your recruiting needs.

iv. Sourcing from professional relationships, customers, associations, vendors, and former employees. This is another winner, but, like iii above, someone needs to remind people frequently of your needs. If you have a significant volume of recruiting needs, this should not be your preferred course of action.

v. LinkedIn has become an indispensable recruiting tool. Everyone uses it. The other social media services and job boards aren't worth much.

vi. Advertising on Craigslist and in classified ads. This is not usually productive, especially for senior-level positions.

vii. Databases of resumes: There are a variety of them floating around; you probably will not get any benefit from them.

viii.All of the above will generate a vast amount of data, most of it irrelevant. There has never been a shortage of resumes. Now, with so many wonderful technology improvements you can easily be overwhelmed by a deluge of information.

VIII. **How to Choose a Search Firm**

If you decide to conduct a retained search, how do you choose a firm? The best way is to build a trusting relationship with a recruiter who knows your business. You don't need to know the entire universe; one or two expert recruiters will do. Obviously the time to build this relationship with a recruiter is before you need one. However, if you don't have such a relationship, pay attention to the following:

a. EXPERIENCE: The search professional should know both your industry and the functional area. It is also surprisingly useful for the recruiter to know you, your company, and your corporate culture.

b. ACCESS: When you hire a recruiter, you expect to gain access to key talent. That's the critical service you are buying. Make sure your recruiter has made it his/her business to know the key people in the industry. In addition to asking about the person's recent search experience, mention prominent people in the industry to make sure he/she knows who they are. Ask specifically about their contacts and relationships in the market.

c. HANDS ON: You should have confidence that the person you hire will actually be doing the work. Some search firms, mostly large ones, bring the subject matter expert in to land the assignment but delegate the actual work to someone junior. If this sounds like a bait and switch, it is.

d. **REFERENCES:** A search firm should have relevant, up-to-date references you can check.

e. **OFF-LIMITS:** Search firms cannot poach candidates from their clients. In taking on a search, the firm usually commits to keeping the company off-limits for a year. Eliminate firms that cannot go into many of your key targets because of client relationships. This is especially important in industries dominated by a few large competitors. Dealing with this is delicate. If a search firm has no clients that are off-limits, they have no relevant experience. On the other hand, too many off-limits constraints will hamper the search, leaving the search firm with few companies to target. Find the middle ground. Large search firms are often severely hampered because they have so many existing client relationships. Because their client lists grow unwieldy, large firms frequently define off-limits in funny ways: rather than declaring the entire company off-limits, only particular departments or divisions will be declared out of bounds. You must decide what is acceptable, but get a clearly defined list of companies from which your recruiter is unable to recruit. Also find out how long your organization will remain off-limits and whether the commitment includes the whole company or only certain divisions. An off-limits guarantee of one year after completion of the search is the norm.

f. **TRUST:** There are plenty of sleazy, incompetent headhunters. Find someone you trust. There is no barrier to entry in executive recruiting, and many practitioners are not particularly gifted, especially at the hard work of placing countless calls and e-mails to find your slate of candidates. The recruiter you choose will be representing your company in the marketplace. Find someone who can do so with intelligence and integrity. Work with someone who will improve your company's brand in the market by representing you effectively and attractively. Since this recruiter will represent you in the marketplace, work with someone who will communicate regularly with candidates and treat them with respect. Even if they are not finalists for the search, candidates still deserve regular communication and feedback.

g. RAPPORT: Find someone you like. You will be spending quite a bit of time with this person.

h. HALO EFFECT: Be loyal to the individual recruiter, not to the firm. Having a good (or bad) experience with one recruiter tells you almost nothing about the rest of the firm. There are good recruiters in big firms and small ones.

i. BIG VERSUS SMALL FIRMS: You will typically get better service, including more of the senior partner's time, by working with small boutique firms that specialize in your industry. This is because the business models are quite different. A small firm is like a narrow pyramid with the partner usually more engaged in the execution of the search. A large firm is like a pyramid with a fat base. It has more resources, but the senior partner is expected to be spending time selling more business, not servicing yours. If you value the expertise of the senior person, you are going to get much more of it with a small firm. However, there may be political pressures to lean towards a large firm. Just as no one ever got fired for hiring IBM, the same is true for hiring a big, brand name search firm.

j. **Shootouts:** This is the least effective way to select a firm, but it may be necessary if you don't have a trusting relationship with a recruiter. Invite two or three firms to make one-hour presentations. Then choose the best. This is a common practice, but all you learn in a shootout is which firm gives the best presentation, not which one delivers the best service.

IX. **How to Manage the Search Firm**

a. **WRITE IT DOWN:** Make sure you have a written agreement, especially on fees, when they are due, and all guarantees. Most firms will expect you to sign a contract to codify the terms of the agreement.

b. **UPDATES:** The search firm should be prepared to provide regular updates. Weekly ones are best. They are usually conducted via phone at regularly scheduled times. During the first couple of weeks of the search, the firm is gearing up and scouring the marketplace for candidates, so don't bother. After the first couple of weeks, the updates are very useful and should include an e-mailed report featuring prospective candidates. Many clients delegate this responsibility to HR, but it is more effective when the hiring manager participates. This allows you to understand how much progress has been made. You will also get a glimmer of the quality of candidates being uncovered.

c. **COMMUNICATIONS TO THE RECRUITER:** A search will move along more quickly and have a much greater chance of success if you, the hiring managing, are prepared to communicate regularly, return calls promptly, and find the answers to questions. Quick responses are particularly useful in keeping a contingency recruiter motivated, since that person may have a variety of potential hires and no guarantee of making a fee on any of them.

d. COMMUNICATIONS FROM THE RECRUITER TO THE MARKETPLACE: Insist that your recruiters show respect to the candidates they talk with in the marketplace. The recruiter is under pressure to deliver you a slate of candidates. It saves time if the recruiter just drops communication with candidates who don't make the cut. That may be efficient, but it is unprofessional. Make sure he/she treats people with respect. This includes regular updates, quick replies, and signing them off if they aren't going to get the job. Lapses in headhunter behavior will make you look bad, and you may not even be aware of it. If the recruiter is an extension of your brand, make sure they burnish that brand by treating people with respect. Likewise, make sure the people on the phone talking to the market are smart and well informed. The partner on the search will not be making every call. There are more junior people at every recruiting firm who are called candidate developers. Since you are paying for the service, it is reasonable for you to ask who will be representing you in the market and whether they will do so in a way that reflects well on you and your company. Many candidate developers are poorly paid and badly informed; some merely read a script. How they are supposed to do an effective job identifying and screening candidates is a mystery.

e. CANDIDATES: A retained search firm should be able to provide four qualified candidates within four to five weeks of launching the search. Hold them to that standard. A contingency firm, working primarily from their existing files, may be able to introduce candidates more quickly, but do not expect them to be carefully vetted. And don't expect much additional work from the contingency firm beyond this initial salvo.

f. DURATION: The entire search process should last two to three months, assuming you and other key participants in the hiring process make yourselves available for interviews.

g. CANDIDATE FLOW: Some clients want to see candidates just as soon as they are identified. Others prefer to wait until the entire slate is assembled. The first version may be necessary if you are in a hurry. If possible, wait until the recruiter has the chance to scour the market and present you with the best candidates available. The candidates unearthed during the first week or two of the search may not pass muster after the recruiter has a chance to compare them to the rest of the marketplace. There may also be a lapse in time between interviewing the first candidate and seeing the rest, during which your memory of the first one may fade. It is far better to schedule the interviews close together.

h. ORDER OF INTERVIEWING: No good recruiter will schedule the best candidate first. The first one you interview sets the bar. It makes no sense to set the bar too high.

i. BENCHMARK CANDIDATES: Early in the search the recruiter may find a pretty good but not outstanding candidate. It may make sense for you to meet that candidate, understanding that he/she is not perfect. This is a nice test to ensure that you and the recruiter share a common understanding of the search. This only works when you and the recruiter trust each other. The recruiter will tell you the plusses and minuses of the benchmark candidate. If you agree after meeting the candidate, that is a very good sign. It means that you are both assessing candidates in the same way.

j. **CLIENT AVAILABILITY:** Hiring managers can't help it. They promise this recruitment is their top priority and then disappear once the search is underway, only to reappear to blame the search firm when the process fails. Client availability is essential for the success of the project. Lack of availability of key members of the client's management team is one of the most frequent causes for a delay in closing the search. With some clients it can be an impediment to getting the search done at all. Anything that you, the hiring manager, can do to police the team assigned to interview candidates can mean the difference between success and failure. Usually the hiring manager is the key decision maker. Problems can follow if too much power is vested in HR to manage the search without regular involvement of the hiring manager.

k. **DECISION MAKING:** Who is the client, the hiring manager or HR? The answer varies with the company. Granted, HR won't make the hiring decision, but decide up front if they will manage the search on a day-to-day basis. It obviously takes work off your desk if they handle the search, but if you lose touch with the process then you lose control and quality may deteriorate. Sorry, you can't entirely hand over responsibility for the search. Sometimes HR gets very jealous of their power and restricts the recruiter's access to you, the hiring manager. This is dangerous. The hiring manager needs to be an active participant throughout the process. The worst obstacles to progress are the so-called "centers of excellence," centralized staffing offices, usually established for budgetary reasons. They tend to be out of touch with the needs of the specific hiring managers; they don't understand the business needs and should not lead the process without regular input from the hiring manager.

I. CONFIDENTIALITY: You are perfectly within your rights as a client to insist that the search remain confidential, meaning that your recruiters will contact prospective candidates without identifying your organization as the client. The only real reason to insist upon confidentiality is if there is an incumbent in the role, making it too risky to inform that person of the search, at least until it is concluded and you have the replacement ready to start. This is a difficult issue, both ethically and practically. Doing a "blind" search, one that does not identify the client, is more difficult. It is much harder for the recruiter to generate excitement about the job and many capable candidates won't talk if you can't identify the client. Of course there are gradations of confidentiality. At the most conservative level, you can forbid your recruiters from identifying your organization at all, even during interviews. This is extreme and unlikely to provide a particularly talented slate of candidates. On the other hand, you can permit your recruiters to identify the client once an initial screening has been completed and the candidate has been sworn to secrecy. This is more common and much more workable. It still hampers the recruiting process, however, particularly if your organization has a sexy brand or is in an attractive period of growth. On occasion, it is understandable that a hiring manager must insist upon confidentiality. But it begs an important question: if the person's contributions are so valuable that you can't get along without him/her, why are you firing him/her in the first place? When launching a confidential search, simply make certain that you really need the incumbent's contributions and aren't just postponing the awkward conversation that will lead to his/her departure. Many confidential searches just don't need to be confidential.

m. FIRING THE RECRUITER: As the client, you can fire the search consultant at any time if you are not satisfied with the quality of the work. The most appropriate time to fire the recruiter is after the first or the second month. This way you can save paying a retainer or two. If you haven't seen resumes at the end of the first month, perhaps you should discuss it with the firm, but you should not terminate the search. If you still haven't seen decent candidates at the end of the second month, you are quite justified in firing them. The problem is that the search still needs to be completed, and you have sunk quite a bit of time and money into the process already. It is a judgment call, but at the very least you should make the firm aware of your displeasure.

X. **Creating a Target List**

a. **Be scientific:** Before you start calling people, decide what sort of companies you want to penetrate. Make a list of relevant target companies. If you hire a search firm, they will do this for you, but make sure you see the target list and agree on the direction of the search. This is important; failure to create a roadmap can easily lead to an unsuccessful, unfilled search. A target list ought to be large, containing dozens of companies, unless you work in a very consolidated industry. Be as flexible as possible to allow lots of contacts. This will allow you to see the best candidates.

b. **Industry experience:** One of your first decisions will be whether you really need candidates to possess relevant industry experience. As a rule, line positions that generate revenue will need industry experience, whereas staff positions such as HR and legal will not. However, the exceptions to this rule probably outnumber the examples of it. Make a decision and stick with it. There is a temptation to be very broad-minded at the beginning of the search, insisting that candidates can come from almost anywhere. Then, toward the end of the search clients can become more conservative, insisting that specific industry experience is required. Changing the rules during the search costs valuable time, rendering many of your candidates unqualified.

c. SIZE OF THE COMPANY: Perhaps even more important than finding candidates with industry experience is finding those who can navigate companies of your approximate size. Operating successfully within a large company is dramatically different from doing so in a small one, and few people can switch seamlessly between the two. This is much more important than it seems on the surface. Most people who thrive in a start-up environment will drown in a large company and vice versa. When creating your target list of companies, keep this in mind and focus on those that are roughly the same size as yours.

d. GEOGRAPHY: The key decision you need to make at this point is whether you will be looking for candidates locally or nationally. This depends on a variety of issues, most importantly the relevant base of talent in your local community. If you are uncertain about whether there is enough local talent to choose from, you may want to begin the search locally and then expand nationally if necessary. You should be able to gather this information within a couple of weeks of launching the search. Your company may have restrictions about paying for relocation, which will certainly govern your geographic targets. Senior-level recruitments frequently do not have geographic constraints, whereas junior-level ones do.

XI. **Where Do Those Candidates Come From, Anyway?**

a. Database: Every recruiter will have a database of prior contacts. Those contacts will be coded according to various criteria such as industry, functional area, and geography. Identifying all the relevant people in the recruiter's database takes no time at all. Large firms (rather predictably) have larger databases than small ones. This is a consideration, but not an overwhelming one in choosing a recruiter. If you choose a recruiter who works regularly in your industry, that person will possess enough people in the database to get going. Keep in mind the database is only a first step. Every search requires original work. Relying exclusively on the database is the sign of a lazy, ineffective recruiter.

b. Prior search records: This resource is intimately related to the database above. The records of all people who were contacted on prior searches will reside in the database. All the notes from all the conversations will be there too, so a recruiter who has recent relevant work experience will have an enormous advantage. A database that doesn't contain recent, relevant searches includes only resumes of people who are actively looking for jobs.

c. Targeted sourcing: This is what most retained recruiters do best. A list of targeted companies is identified; the recruiter or a member of the research staff will then identify all the relevant executives at the right level within that company. The recruiter or a member of the staff will contact the executive to ascertain whether that person could be interested. It pays to have someone who is very, very good on the phone to make those pitches. The work is boring, but if it is left to someone who is junior or unqualified then you will be unable to convert top-quality executives into candidates for your search.

d. REFERRALS: A recruitment works best when the recruiter is able to call senior-level executives, usually a step or two higher than the role you are trying to fill, and ask who the best people in the marketplace are for an assignment. This provides you with a valuable endorsement from a prominent industry executive, which is irreplaceable. This is also the most difficult avenue because the senior executives are unlikely to return calls unless they know and trust the recruiter. Headhunters who are well known and well placed in your industry obviously have a huge advantage in being able to exploit these references.

e. LINKEDIN: What an amazing tool! It is highly useful, and everyone uses it. LinkedIn doesn't replace good judgment, but it provides unbelievable access. LinkedIn has already decimated the ranks of lower-level contingency recruiters. Internal recruiters now find they have such wonderful access that the contingency recruiters and their databases are no longer necessary. Senior-level recruiters have not been adversely affected, probably because senior searches have many moving parts, whereas lower-level ones are more straightforward, almost commodities. LinkedIn cannot (yet) identify candidates for senior searches where the list of requirements is as long as your arm and many of those requirements are not featured on the resume. Their technologists are undoubtedly working on it. My hope is they won't be successful until after I retire.

f. **MANY, MANY CALLS:** A good recruiter will make perhaps hundreds of calls in the course of a search. An old headhunter rule of thumb is that it requires one hundred well-targeted calls to yield four qualified candidates, which results in a successfully completed search. Frankly, it often requires much more than one hundred calls.

XII. Evaluating Resumes

a. REVIEWING RESUMES: There has never been a shortage resumes. With the use of e-mails and social media, there are now thousands. Decide up front who should be carrying the load of reviewing all the resumes, the hiring manager, HR, or the search firm. If a search firm has been hired, the answer is easy. You, the client, should only be reviewing resumes of candidates that have been screened and who meet the specifications. If the firm is retained, each candidate should have been interviewed personally, and you should have a write-up that illuminates matters not discussed on the resume. Contingency firms may submit backgrounds that are on target, but don't count on it. You will need to oversee their work carefully.

b. PACE YOURSELF: If you are reviewing resumes on your own, keep in mind that even the strongest brains will turn to mush after too many resumes. Read a few and make notes, jot down your questions, but don't even dream that you can intelligently review dozens at a single sitting.

c. WHAT A RESUME SHOULD LOOK LIKE:

   i. It should be no more than two pages.

   ii. It should be chronological. In recent years outplacement counselors have urged job candidates, especially those with career gaps they want to hide, to adopt alternative formats, the most common of which is the "skills" or "functional" resume. Even the most perceptive reader cannot make sense of them. Many people use this format even when they are not trying to hide something, but they possess an unusual career trajectory or career changes. This is still unacceptable. When faced with a fancy resume, insist the candidate submit a chronological one.

iii. It should feature "action words." Some passive language ("was responsible for…") is unavoidable, but the most prominent features should be accomplishments that are measurable.

iv. Most resumes feature a summary of experience at the top. This is usually useless. Resume writers should skip the platitudes and say something specific about the sort of job they are actually looking for and/or the value they will provide to the employer. If done correctly, the summary can be helpful to the reader.

d. WHAT TO LOOK FOR:

i. Keep the job description nearby to remind you of the key agenda points. The best way to read resumes is to create a form with these "must have" points entered neatly in the left column. Leave the right column blank to allow you to jot notes on how the candidate meets these specs. This is a good trick to make sure you keep the big picture in mind and judge each resume by a common standard.

ii. Achievements, especially those that are relevant to the job at hand and can be quantitatively measured (e.g., improved sales by 14 percent). The best indicator of future success is past success.

iii. Upward mobility, especially repeated promotions within a single company. This is important.

iv. Has the candidate changed jobs too often or too infrequently? Average tenure at a company has declined steadily over the past fifty years. Still, a lot of jumps in a resume reflect badly on the person's effectiveness and staying power. Quick moves early in someone's career are to be expected. Not so after a few years. Conversely, many years at a single company may make you wonder if the candidate can adapt to another corporate culture. More than fifteen years will certainly give you pause. Large companies like IBM and Procter & Gamble are fabulous places, but they are so rigidly structured that their alumni often find it difficult to adapt to new cultures.

e. **INDUSTRY EXPERIENCE:** In reviewing candidates, be clear about whether industry experience is necessary. In staff jobs (HR, finance) it often is not. Even in line jobs (sales), it frequently helps to expand the pool of talent by including candidates from outside the industry, especially if your industry has grown inbred. Industry experience can reduce start-up time, it is true, but try to think of the long term and hire the strongest candidate with the most potential. An important exception: highly technical jobs are another story and may strictly require relevant industry experience.

f. COMPANY SIZE: Moving from a large company to a small one is difficult. Same thing with moving from small to large. The ways things get done, the amount of resources, the methods of communication, the necessary style of management are all very different. Most people fail if they try to move abruptly between big and small. Furthermore, many of them are unaware they have a sweet spot and have made their career choices entirely at a visceral level. It is not unusual for executives from a Fortune 50 company, for example, to seek out a promising start-up. Most of the time they fail miserably, having been used to an entirely different level of resources and structure. In reviewing resumes, keep your eyes peeled for candidates with experience in companies of a similar size to yours.

g. THEORY: Develop a hypothesis/set of expectations about the candidate to be proven or disproven in the interview.

h. LIES: It is very difficult to determine whether a candidate is lying (or exaggerating a bit) on the resume. It is helpful to underline suspicious claims so you can discuss them in the interview. One of the most frequent areas of deception is education. Fortunately degrees can be checked easily, and doing so should be standard operating procedure. Another frequent area of exaggeration is compensation. This will not be on the resume, but if you suspect you are not hearing the truth, ask for W-2 forms. In reality, few companies request confirmation of compensation, but catching a candidate in a lie reveals a serious character weakness, and you should eliminate this candidate promptly.

i. GAPS IN THE RESUME: Finding a new job can take a long time, up to a year, especially for senior executives. A gap in the resume is not necessarily a knockout, but it certainly merits investigation.

j. MAKE NOTES: From reading the resume, jot notes about concerns, issues, or theories to be discussed directly with the candidate. There may, for example, be sound reasons behind frequent career moves.

k. LIMITATIONS OF THE RESUME: You can't judge a candidate from a resume. Period. The best you can do is to make an educated judgment about whether to move to the next step. Those who try to draw far-reaching conclusions from a few typewritten pages aren't recruiting effectively and do the candidates an injustice.

l. FOREIGN-BASED CANDIDATES: I receive a steady stream of resumes from foreign countries looking for jobs in the United States. Often these are Americans who have accepted an international assignment and find themselves stuck overseas. These people are in a pickle. No client wants to fly someone in from another continent for an interview. If the candidate is a non-US citizen without work papers, the objections are even greater. Not only is it a hassle to interview the person, arranging for visas is even worse. Clients simply refuse to deal with it. Candidates from Canada are viewed more favorably, although obtaining a visa is still an issue.

XIII. **Diversity**

a. FIT: Finding new employees that fit the corporate culture is an essential part of your job. Nobody fits in every corporate culture. As an astute hiring manager, you will want to develop an understanding of what sort of person succeeds in your company. The more senior the position you have to fill, the more important this is. Lower-level jobs may be filled by putting a square peg into a square hole. Not so with a senior-level role, where communication and relationships are more critical to success. The problem with this is that people tend to hire others who look and act exactly like they do. They want people who wear the same starched white shirt or perhaps the same black T-shirt. What's wrong with this? Well, for one, it winds up being discriminatory and potentially illegal. Secondly, it fails to take advantage of the abilities and experiences of an increasingly diverse work force. Consequently, virtually all American companies embrace the goal of diversity, or at least give it lip service. Embracing diversity while finding executives who will fit within your corporate culture means that you, the hiring manager, need to work harder. You need to look beyond the superficial trappings of what defines the corporate culture to what attributes are genuinely important. One important bit of advice: If you have goals of increasing the racial or gender diversity within your organization, establish your expectations clearly with your recruiters at the outset of the search. Make sure you are on the same page with HR too. It sometimes winds up that HR emphasizes the importance of diversity whereas the hiring manager doesn't care at all.

b. RACE: This is a daunting topic. So much has been written about the pursuit of racial diversity in the work force that I question whether I have anything new to contribute. However, it is remarkable that while every company purports to have a diversity agenda, the goal is pursued in remarkably different ways. In some cases it is not mentioned at all during the search, whereas other clients make it a priority from the outset. As the hiring manager, you define the rules, including a precise description of what diversity means. Usually clients ask for African American and Hispanic candidates when they request diversity. However, different companies face different challenges. Furthermore, clarify whether you are asking for a diverse slate of candidates to provide a choice or whether you will consider only diversity candidates.

c. WOMEN: Although they remain underrepresented in top management, women have unquestionably made huge strides gaining access to the executive ranks. It is interesting, however, how uneven progress has been across different functional areas. Sales, marketing, human resources, and other staff groups have seemingly opened their doors to women. Less so in finance, technology, and operations. Very odd. One would think that attentive employers would try to rectify this imbalance. By now everyone should have noticed that companies tend to function more smoothly with an ample representation of both genders.

d. **OLDER CANDIDATES:** Another area in which I have seen a shift in behavior is the hiring of older candidates. Twenty-five years ago, most companies were not interested in candidates older than forty-five years. Today clients are receptive to candidates in their fifties and even sixties. There are several trends behind this:

    i. A significant war for talent is underway, making candidates with scarce skill sets particularly desirable.

    ii. Baby boomers, despite their increasing age, still outnumber succeeding generations by a considerable margin.

    iii. Improving health in older workers allows them to be productive longer.

    iv. Greater open-mindedness among employers.

    v. Older workers often bring stability and wisdom. Because finding a new job is difficult, they tend to be loyal, which can be a valuable attribute.

    vi. Hiring older workers has certain liabilities, which means that employers must exercise caution:

        1. Extra care must be taken to make sure that an older worker will fit in. There have been instances where older workers insist that a particular way of doing things is the way they've always done it. This sort of rigidity does not make for helpful collaboration.

2. Older workers often do not possess the technical skills of younger generations. This will be more or less important depending on how technical the job is.

3. Do they possess the health and energy to do a great job?

4. While these are legitimate concerns, it should be clear to the reader that the advantages of hiring older workers outweigh the liabilities. A little bit of probing during the interview process should allow you to hire only those workers with the energy, flexibility, and technical skills to flourish.

5. Despite the progress that has been made, older workers face huge obstacles to employment. Corporations are typically shaped like a pyramid. The higher one gets on the pyramid, the fewer blocks there are to occupy. When an executive gets bumped off the pyramid, it is difficult to reenter, especially if the employee is over fifty-five. With the growing scarcity of talent in this country, companies simply will have to find ways to readmit older workers who are healthy, capable, and eager to work. Perhaps these candidates will have to take a step backward on the pyramid, but for many older workers this will be quite acceptable, especially if it is combined with some flexibility on workload and hours spent in the office. This is going to change the way hiring is done,

but it is silly, not to mention discriminatory, to squander all that talent.

e. **YOUNGER WORKERS:** Millennials, those entering the work force around the turn of the century, have been subjected to all sorts of negative press. Critics call them entitled, narcissistic, materialistic, and unwilling to work hard. This is a pretty damning indictment, especially for an entire generation. If any of these generalizations are true, I suspect they will subside when the millennials, also known as Gen Y, get a few gray hairs and start families of their own. It is an unassailable fact, however, that younger workers tend to be impatient and move more frequently between jobs. Almost anyone's resume probably contains a few forgettable, choppy stints at the beginning of one's career before settling into a pattern of growth and stability.

   i. Younger workers are much more likely to be technologically adept, and they possess abundant energy.

   ii. To put these skills to work, employers may have to offer compromises. The most obvious place to compromise is in offering greater flexibility in where and when the work gets done. Some work environments will lend themselves more to this sort of flexibility than others.

f. **RETURNING WORKERS:** This represents the greatest untapped source of talent in the economy: people who have stepped out of the work force for some years and who are eager to step back in. Most frequently, this is the domain of women who have taken time away from work to raise families, but it is in no way limited to that group. It does, however, represent a huge opportunity and a huge problem for most companies. As mentioned above in the discussion of older workers, most corporations are structured like pyramids; once one gets off the pyramid it is very difficult to get back on, especially at senior levels. This is silly and a huge missed opportunity. A woman's skills are unlikely to deteriorate after a few years out of the work force. While it sounds like an easy matter to fix, it will actually require real structural change in American corporations for that to happen.

XIV. **Phone Screens**

a. THE IMPORTANCE OF A PHONE SCREEN: Although not essential, a fifteen-minute phone call with the likely candidates can save valuable time. By speaking with the candidates before inviting them for an interview, you may be able to eliminate some, saving time and money, especially if they would have to travel long distances. If you trust your recruiter, don't bother with spending the time on the phone screen. If you are doing the recruitment yourself, on the other hand, go ahead.

b. Phone interviews often need to be performed in the evening, as the candidate may not have time or privacy in the office. With the increasing popularity of open-office formats, confidential discussions with candidates can be difficult at work.

c. Use the phone screen for a technical evaluation, not to assess chemistry. Look at the list of must-have qualifications to determine the person's ability to do the job. The phone screen should be short. Once you have determined if the candidate is qualified, get off the phone. Save the more complicated assessments for the face-to-face interview. The amount of data you can collect about fit and chemistry is far greater in person.

XV. **Preparing for the Interview**

a. HOW MANY CANDIDATES: After reviewing resumes and conducting phone screens, winnow the list of potential candidates down to a manageable number, say four, to bring in for face-to-face interviews. Four candidates will provide you with alternatives, yet this isn't an overwhelming number. If the candidates do not live up to expectations, add more later.

b. COMPENSATION EXPECTATIONS: Before candidates are asked to come in for interviews, be certain someone has talked openly about compensation. Your recruiters should not be presenting you with candidates who are not priced appropriately for the job. This means there needs to be room within your compensation parameters to provide a worthwhile increase. This does not mean you should be negotiating compensation with the candidates at this early juncture; just make sure you are not wasting your time. This sounds obvious, but it is a rule that is often violated or neglected. Occasionally a candidate will be well into the interview process before anyone discovers he/she is unaffordable. This is a serious oversight. Sometimes a candidate will consider a lateral move, especially if unemployed, but this must be discussed openly at the outset of your conversations. Even before the first interview.

c. THE INTERVIEW SCHEDULE: An executive-level position often requires three rounds of interviews, not including the phone screen if you conducted one. For more junior jobs, a single round of interviews will probably suffice. Even for quite senior jobs, don't be seduced into demanding six or seven interviews. Some clients claim they need to conduct myriad interviews to achieve what they call "buy in." This can ruin the search and will take forever. No candidate will please everyone. Keep your interview panel as small as possible or you may never complete the hire.

d. THE MECHANICS OF INTERVIEWING:

    i. Scheduling: It can be a nightmare to schedule interviews, especially if the candidate is employed and you are jockeying for time with busy executives from your company. Good support staff is essential for getting the meetings arranged. Schedule only one candidate to come in at a time, or do it carefully if you really need to bring in several at once. It will be embarrassing if they bump into each other. Conversely, don't let weeks pass between interviews. You will forget the first one by the time you meet the second.

    ii. Write it down: Before the candidate arrives, make a written record of the candidate's interview schedule. Make sure everyone on the list has a copy of it and is prepared to adhere to the timetable.

    iii. Avoid group interviews.

iv. Identify in advance all skills and experiences that are essential to doing the job successfully, as well as those that would be nice to have.

v. Review the resume as well as any other available write-ups and LinkedIn bios. Form a hypothesis about the person that will be proven or disproven during the interview.

vi. Prepare some questions (see below). Make sure they pertain to the job description.

vii. Interviews work best when they are structured, but not rigidly so. Have clear goals to achieve. You are not simply talking to these people to get to know them. Each candidate should be held to the same standard and asked approximately the same questions.

viii. Don't conduct a first interview over a meal. Eating is a distraction.

ix. Be on time; don't make the candidate wait.

x. Plan a smooth transition between interviews to create a positive interview experience for the candidates. Assign someone, perhaps an administrative assistant, to take the candidates from one office to another or, if interviewing in a conference room, to make sure the next interviewer comes promptly when the prior meeting is completed.

xi. Assign someone to take the candidate to lunch, debrief at the end of the interviews, walk the candidate to the door, and say good-bye. The importance of these last three points cannot be overstated. They seem trivial, but candidates will judge you harshly if they are not handled efficiently.

e. ASSEMBLE THE INTERVIEW TEAM:

  i. Don't get carried away. The hiring manager and the relevant member of your HR team are probably the only ones who should interview in the first round. And perhaps include a trusted peer. If you are thinking of adding others, talk to them first. Make sure they know what is important, perhaps by providing them the list of key skills described above. Interview training, either by HR or an outside executive recruiter (or simply by reading this book), is readily available. Lousy interviewers will fail to provide useful feedback and might even alienate attractive candidates.

  ii. Keep the jury to a minimum. Under the guise of gaining "consensus," some clients try to involve too many people on the interview schedule. This is a mistake. People who are tangential to the process will not interview carefully and will probably only judge whether the candidate is likeable. Some people may even possess a different agenda that will undermine your efforts. Others pride themselves on being tough and will reject almost everyone. The more people you put on the interview schedule, the greater the risk that capable candidates will be needlessly eliminated and that you may lose control of the process.

iii. Make sure participants on the interview schedule take their roles seriously. Tell them what you hope to achieve by making this hire and ask them to review the candidate's background in advance.

iv. Be sure to communicate the importance of a positive attitude during the interview. An enthusiastic demeanor can make the difference in attracting a highly desirable candidate. Interviewers who are distracted or who lack conviction can spoil the process. Get them off the interviewing schedule.

v. If you wait until the last moment to ask colleagues to interview, this guarantees that the newly appointed interviewer will do a lousy job. The best feedback you are likely to get from a last-minute interview is "yeah, I liked him" or some other vague reaction based on gut feel.

vi. It can be helpful to assign a role to each interviewer that includes areas and questions to be covered. This reduces the chance that each interviewer will cover the same boring territory.

vii. Take notes: Use the same form you created in evaluating resumes with the key agenda points on the left and on the right the ways the candidates meet those points. Make some notes on physical appearance to remind you later which candidate is which. Otherwise, after a week or so, they will all blur together.

f. CHOOSE A LOCATION:

    i.   Interviews may be conducted in your office or a conference room, depending on the condition and availability of both.

    ii.   If you conduct the interview in your office, clean up a bit. Your mess can be distracting, and it sends the wrong message. Be aware of the power dynamics and do not put the interviewee at a disadvantage by talking across a big desk. Comfortable chairs work; sitting side by side on a couch is too intimate and should be avoided. You should offer a neat, comfortable, relaxed atmosphere free of distractions. Take a look around and see what your office says about you and your company and make sure you are putting your best foot forward. Put your phone on "Do Not Disturb" and avoid interruptions. Be polite and offer something to drink.

    iii.   A conference room is more neutral, which can be good or bad depending on what your office looks like. A neutral conference room is preferable to a crummy office but not to a nice, comfortable one that communicates some personality.

    iv.   You can move the candidates around from office to office or put them in a central conference room and have the interviewers come to them.

g. TO SELL OR NOT TO SELL:

    i.   Yes, sell. Go ahead and sell! Be enthusiastic about the challenge and your company. The primary goal of the interview is to allow you to assess the candidate's qualifications, but an important secondary goal is to build the candidate's excitement about the opportunity. Keep in mind that the candidates are assessing you, just as you are assessing them. Especially if you have found an attractive candidate, don't hesitate to express your enthusiasm. Most clients have an intuitive understanding of how to behave during an interview. Be enthusiastic, lean forward, connect with the candidate.

ii. Under no circumstances should you exaggerate or misrepresent the opportunity. You simply should represent why this job is exciting.

iii. Don't brag: Talking about yourself isn't the same as selling the job. It is the mark of an inexperienced interviewer to talk excessively about one's self. Frankly, this reveals more about the insecurity of the interviewer than anything else. You don't need to brag to establish yourself as a person of responsibility. Don't offer a step-by-step description of your career. The key reason to discuss your own experiences is to identify things you have in common with the candidate. Nothing creates a solid connection with another person like a common experience.

iv. The worst client is the one who believes he/she doesn't have to sell. One of my clients felt it was beneath her to display any excitement about the job. Her view was that the candidates were there to sell her. She became irate at the suggestion that she should help to sell the opportunity and was offended that several candidates withdrew from consideration after the interview because they did not want to work for her. Needless to say, this was not my easiest or most pleasant assignment.

XVI. Different Interviews for Different Jobs

Your approach to an interview will vary depending on the functional area. Interviewing a sales executive is very different from a controller. Here are some tips about interviewing candidates in various key functional areas:

a. GENERAL MANAGEMENT: Candidates for these most senior positions should have significant presence. They should be unflappable and convey confidence. After all, they are expected to be the leaders of the business. Their conversation should be peppered with anecdotes about successful strategies they've employed and illustrations of how they have built the business. These examples should be expressed in measurable terms (improved sales by 20 percent; decreased operating expenses by 20 percent, etc.). Experience managing a P&L is expected.

b. SALES: Interviewing sales executives is either easy or difficult, depending on how you view it. Salespeople view an interview as a sales pitch. The product just happens to be them. If they don't have the skills to build rapport with you, the interview should be a short one. Interviewing salespeople is usually enjoyable, but it can be difficult to tell when you are being "sold." When asking for performance measures, which is essential, make sure the candidate answers the question, since good salespeople will know a dozen ways to frame an answer to describe themselves in the most flattering light. It is critical to determine if the candidate is able to:

   i.   Handle rejection and overcome objections.

   ii. Listen, understand a client's business problems, and identify solutions that your products/services can offer.

   iii. Understand the steps that go into solutions selling.

   iv. Capable of role-playing to demonstrate selling skills.

   v. Able to cite examples of

      a. Having failed to meet expectations.

      b. Creatively closed a sale that was on the brink of disaster.

      c. Identifying where his/her performance ranks versus peers.

      d. What he/she likes and dislikes about selling.

      e. How he/she feels about travel.

      f. How he/she manages time, what a typical day looks like.

      g. How much he/she values teamwork and cooperation.

c. **TECHNOLOGY:** A lot of technologists choose their career because they prefer dealing with technology to dealing with people. Even many senior-level IT executives possess poor interpersonal skills. You can't judge an IT executive by the same interview standards as a general management candidate. When interviewing junior engineering roles, the conversation will be highly technical. Candidates must be screened by members of your team who are technically adept and understand the culture of your company and its business goals. Frankly, senior-level interviews are easier. By the time an IT exec is being considered for a CTO or CIO role, this person should be able to speak some semblance of English. Their conversation should be filled with examples of how they have used technology to achieve business goals. They should understand the business strategy of their current company and their role in achieving it.

d. **FINANCE:** Like IT executives, financial executives are often highly technical and are not blessed with effervescent interpersonal skills. Unlike IT executives, there are many exceptions to this rule. Those who do have strong interpersonal skills have a good chance of ascending into general management. If you are not a financial executive yourself, you will be surprised at how different the skills and experiences are between treasury, control, and financial planning and analysis. These days, the best candidates for CFO come from the controllers' ranks, FP&A, or, better yet, some combination of the two.

e. **OPERATIONS:** This will include such functions as manufacturing, logistics, warehousing, distribution, order fulfillment, procurement, and the like. Depending on the industry, a career in operations could either be a clear path to the top or a career cul-de-sac. Jobs in operations differ so much from company to company and industry to industry that it doesn't make much sense to offer specific interview advice.

f. **MARKETING**: Marketing pros are supposed to see the big picture. Marketing is about stimulating demand, whereas sales pertains to meeting demand. In consumer packaged goods companies, marketing is considered a line function, whereas in many others it is purely a staff role. On the whole, marketing execs tend to be quite polished. They frequently interview well, but can be incredible BS artists. It is not unusual for a marketing executive to claim credit for every program, project or product he/she has ever touched, so be wary of exaggerated claims.

g. **HUMAN RESOURCES**: HR searches are perhaps the most difficult searches of all. First of all, the importance of the function varies dramatically from company to company and industry to industry. Unless you really know a company, you cannot tell if HR really has a seat at the table. Secondly, all HR executives say pretty much the same bromides about being a "business partner." It is very difficult to ascertain the importance of the HR function and its executives' true role in their current company. The rule of thumb is that HR plays a more powerful, strategic role in larger companies and less so in smaller ones. Exceptions to this rule, however, are extremely numerous.

XVII. **Types of Interviews**

Below is a quick guide to the different forms of interviews. Choose one or incorporate several into your interview style.

    a. STRESS INTERVIEWS: We have all heard about them, but in reality they are rarely used. And with good reason. The underlying reasoning behind stress interviews is that jobs are stressful, so it makes sense to see how a candidate reacts under pressure. Unless you are highly skilled, this is likely to be a bust, and you will probably only alienate the candidate. Most interviews are stressful enough without playing games to put the candidate off balance.

    b. BEHAVIORAL INTERVIEWS: These focus on how the candidate acted in specific situations, given that the best predictor of future performance is past performance. Candidates are encouraged to talk about past initiatives, their thinking, and what they would do if they had it to do over again.

    c. SITUATIONAL INTERVIEWS: Ask candidates to describe their performance or how they would respond to situations they will face on the job. Get each candidate as close as possible to the actual challenges of the job so you can make a sound evaluation. Versions of this style include performing case studies during the interview, analyzing financial statements, and role-playing. For example, ask the interviewee, "What would be your approach to…"

d. SKILLS-BASED INTERVIEWS: These force the interviewer to keep in mind the specific skills and experiences necessary to succeed in this position. This style involves pointed questions about the set of skills possessed by each candidate. Understanding their skills will provide insights into the candidates' motivations and potential fit in the organization. Clever candidates, however, can guess the answers you are seeking to questions such as "tell me about your key strengths" or "what abilities did you use in this situation." Skills-based questions should therefore represent a small portion of your interview time.

e. CHRONOLOGICAL INTERVIEWS: Briefly walking through a candidate's background chronologically provides you with an understanding of *why* the candidates made career decisions, whereas looking at the resume only lets you understand *what* they have done. Chronological interviewing can be effective if you don't let it get out of hand. Allowing the candidate to tell his/her life's story uninterrupted will suck up the entire interview. Encourage the candidate to be brief. Find out why the person made decisions and interrupt to ask behavioral questions to understand what the candidate achieved and how it was accomplished. Examining the person's career track also allows you to discover things you have in common, forming a bond.

f. SUMMARY: The best approach is to rely primarily but not exclusively on behavioral interviewing questions. Situational questions are also useful and so are skills-based ones, especially those that reveal the candidate's career goals. A quick stroll through his/her career chronology can also be useful to understand why the candidate made certain choices. Don't make this the central component of the interview, however.

g. CONSISTENCY: Each interview with each candidate should be conducted the same way. While this does not mean asking exactly the same questions, it does mean using the same yardstick and assessing the same issues, both technical and cultural.

XVIII. **Sample Questions**

Below is a list of sample questions that might be useful. This is NOT an exhaustive list, nor should you even dream of asking all of them. When preparing for an interview, pick a few that are relevant.

  i. What do you want me to remember about you?

  ii. What do you like and dislike about your current/most recent job?

  iii. Describe a situation where you had to convince others to adopt your plan of action (then describe the outcome).

  iv. If your boss is in the process of making a mistake, what are you going to do? Give an example.

  v. Describe your strengths and weaknesses (ask this ONLY for your own amusement, since the answer to the latter part is inevitably some version of "I try too hard" or "I am impatient to achieve success").

  vi. Tell me about how you dealt with a policy or outcome you disagreed with.

vii. Tell me about an instance when you had to work with a difficult peer or boss.

viii. What are you most praised for in your organization? Criticized for?

ix. Give me an example of when you had too much to do (determine ability to prioritize).

x. Tell me about an initiative of yours that did not succeed. What would you have done differently? What did you learn?

xi. Tell me about an experience that best prepares you for the challenge at our company.

xii. Describe a decision or program of yours that was controversial or unpopular.

xiii. What have you done to generate or save money for your company?

xiv. What has been your greatest failure and what have you learned from it? Your greatest success?

xv. What did you learn from your time in prison? (That's a joke; just to see if you are paying attention.)

xvi. In a few words, how would your boss describe you? (Compare this with the actual response from the boss in the reference.)

xvii. How heavy was your workload at the time?

xviii. Tell me the most difficult part of this project and how you dealt with it.

xix. Given all these responsibilities, tell me how you organized your time.

xx. How would you have improved your performance?

xxi. What doesn't your resume tell me about you?

xxii. Of all your bosses, who would give you the strongest/weakest recommendation? Why?

xxiii. What other responsibilities did you have that we have not discussed?

xxiv. Why did you leave your last position (if appropriate)? This often requires serious probing. If the answer is by mutual agreement, find out more. This often is a face-saving version of "I got fired."

XIX. **The First Interview**

i. QUALIFICATIONS: In the first interview, find out if the candidates are truly qualified. Worry less about "fit" issues or about falling in love with the perfect person. This round is devoted to winnowing the pool of candidates to a more manageable number. Try to start with a slate of four candidates. Interview them close together, not necessarily on the same day but close enough to remember the first one when you are meeting the last. If none of the initial candidates proves acceptable, you can go back to develop more. If your recruiters have done their jobs, however, you will usually get close to the bull's-eye with the first group.

ii. SHORTCUT: Let's say the candidate is in the lobby waiting for you, but you've done absolutely nothing to prepare. You feel like a jerk, but what can you do? Here are some quick steps to acquit yourself pretty well:

1. Review the resume.

2. Grab a few interview questions from section XVII.

3. Review the interview outline below:

a. Introduction – Put the candidate at ease.

b. Overview – Provide a brief description of the job and its key challenges.

c. Work history – Ask the candidate to walk through his/her work history. Pick a couple of accomplishments and probe. Ask about his/her personal involvement in the issue, what problems were overcome, what he/she learned.

d. Ask several behavioral questions to reveal the way the candidate acts and reacts in specific projects.

e. Summarize – Relate items from the candidate's background to critical job responsibilities and ask situational questions (what would you do in this situation?).

f. Thank candidate and promise to communicate shortly about next steps.

g. Do a better job of preparing so this doesn't happen again.

iii. FULL INTERVIEW SUMMARY: For those inquisitive souls who want greater detail about conducting an effective interview, this is for you:

1. Be on time. Don't make the candidate wait.

2. Smile, shake hands, offer your business card and water or coffee.

3. Put the candidate at ease: Begin the interview with a couple of minutes of conversation. This is useful to put the candidate at ease and can also establish if this is someone with whom you can develop a future rapport. One easy way to start is to mention something on the candidate's resume that you share in common.

4. Overview: Offer a brief description of the position and its key challenges. Don't make it elaborate. This is not the time to sell, not yet. Keep it simple and quick. Offer more details at the end of the interview to avoid providing information that allows candidates to tailor their answers to what you want to hear.

5. Shut up: This can't be stressed too often. Don't talk too much. Listen. Be quiet. Take notes. Talk no more than one-third of the time

6. Work history: Ask for a brief chronological outline. Candidates will find this easy, and it is therefore a good way to dispel tension and get them talking. Don't let this run on too long. Left to their own devices, candidates will eat up a lot of time telling you about their lives when all you want is some elaboration on their proudest moments. Be prepared to speed the candidate up by interrupting with questions and guidance about the level of detail you seek. Mention that you want to spend only five (or ten) minutes in

this part of the interview. The recitation also allows you to understand why the candidate has changed jobs or made certain choices that may not be evident on the resume. A few questions about what the candidate liked or did not like, or what personal contribution he/she was able to make, can prove insightful. Repeated, probing questions about a relevant experience can be very helpful. The key insight you are looking for in this early part of the search is whether the candidate is qualified to do the job. If the candidate is truly unqualified, you probably will know it by now, permitting you to draw the interview to an early close.

7. In reviewing the work history you are looking for:

   a. Responsibilities

   b. Real contributions and accomplishments and how they were achieved

   c. Knowledge required to do the job

   d. Examples of their judgment and how they handle problems

   e. Scope of responsibility

   f. Management responsibility and skill

8. Results: The candidate should offer measurable results from his/her efforts. Be attentive for

exaggerations or for personally taking credit for the achievements of others. Asking questions like "How much of this was really due to your personal contribution?" will help. If you feel you are being snowed, ask repeatedly about problems and instances where the candidate handled adversity or faced failure. If after all this you have not heard anything other than an unrelenting string of brilliant successes, be suspicious. This is the crux of the interview, where most of the time should be spent. Your questions should be open ended, forcing the candidate to explain thinking and actions. Don't allow a candidate to get away with useless yes or no answers.

9. Keep it simple: Don't string multiple questions together.

10. Organizational structure: Understanding how an executive fits into his/her current company can be difficult, sometimes intentionally so if the candidate is trying to exaggerate. Yet this knowledge is essential to determine the true scope of the candidate's responsibility. Unraveling this can be easy by asking the candidate to describe the organizational structure, including:

   a. where he/she reports in the organization

   b. who else reports to the candidate's boss and how their responsibilities differ from the candidate's

    c. who reports directly to the candidate and what their key responsibilities are

    d. the size of the candidate's total team, including indirect reports

    e. whether the team reports exclusively to the candidate or if there are dotted-line relationships elsewhere

    f. whether the team reports to the candidate permanently or merely on a project basis. It is much more important to hire, fire, and offer performance reviews than merely to oversee a group during a project.

11. Compensation – If an executive recruiter has not provided compensation information for the candidate, it is important to pin it down during the interview. Frankly, this should have been handled before bringing a candidate in to interview. You shouldn't be at the interview stage without complete compensation information.

    a. If you need to ask about compensation, mention up front that you always verify compensation in order to prevent exaggerations.

    b. If a candidate is beyond your financial parameters, tell the candidate and end the conversation. Don't waste time. Occasionally the candidate will have a reason for being willing to accept a lateral or even a step back. A willingness to take a haircut always raises eyebrows, but it pays to listen to the reasoning. There may be a sound explanation, allowing you to hire a more senior executive.

c. Never ask candidates how much they are seeking. That places the power in the hands of the candidate, where it does not belong. An interview, especially a first interview, is not the place to launch a salary negotiation.

12. Personal life:

a. Most hiring managers want to find out about the candidates' lives and interests. This can be delicate. Legally, you can't ask if the person is married or many other things you probably would like to know. If the person starts to talk about his/her personal situation, however, feel free to listen. Probing into the candidate's life has become increasingly controversial. What a person does outside of work, the argument goes, is none of your business and provides grounds for discrimination. Maybe so, but that does not stop many hiring managers from being interested. Since they spend a lot of time with the candidates, hiring managers want to work with interesting people with whom they share a few things in common. Just don't say or do anything that might be considered discriminatory.

b. It is perfectly acceptable to ask what candidates are reading, what sort of media they follow, where they travel. Most executives want to work with people who are naturally curious. Those people tend to read and explore things that enable them to grow.

13. Body language:

a. Yours: Maintain positive body communication. Lean forward, but not too intently. Nod your head and don't interrupt. Your expression should be friendly but without the Cheshire cat grin. Keep your hands away from your face and don't fidget.

b. The candidate: Check to see if the interviewee's body language matches his or her words. You are hoping to see a relaxed, confident demeanor with good eye contact, not someone twisted up like a self-conscious pretzel.

14. Self-awareness: Candidates for senior-level roles should be able to articulate their strengths and weaknesses. They should be self-aware and able to talk openly about them. Insecure people will try to deflect questions about weaknesses; confident leaders will

discuss them openly, but in a way that does not torpedo their candidacies.

15. Getting fired: This is not the big red flag it used to be. Plenty of highly talented, hard-working people get fired. If someone has been fired, you need to explore in order to gain a better understanding of the reasons. Perhaps this will cause dismissal of the candidate from consideration, probably not. If the candidate tries to fib about his/her departure from a company, that is frankly a bigger cause for concern. Catching someone in a lie should end the candidate's candidacy.

16. Career gaps: As with getting fired above, having a gap in one's career is not as damaging as it once was. Simply looking for a job, especially at senior levels, takes time. Finding a new job at the executive level often takes a year, but not more. If a candidate has taken time off for other reasons, such as raising a family or dealing with health issues, let's hope that we all have become sophisticated enough to permit that sort of thing. Talent is too rare to dismiss candidates who don't have a purely linear background.

17. Managerial skill: If the job requires managerial responsibility, questions about the candidate's skills in this area should outweigh specific technical concerns, since the responsibility of a manager is to get the most from the team. It makes sense, therefore, to focus on how

the candidate performs such duties as hiring, firing, and improving the skill sets of his/her team. Key issues include:

a. How the candidates find and keep key members of their team and what they look for. How many people they have actually hired and fired. Have they merely inherited a mature organization or built a team?

b. What other groups and departments they interact with.

c. How they hold the team accountable and maintain discipline.

d. Have they been successful in expanding the skill set of the team and getting its members promoted?

e. How they manage during a crisis.

f. How they motivate the staff; how they improve/retain morale, especially in a time of crisis.

g. What communication style do they prefer? How are goals set and progress monitored? (Hint: an explicit, formal process is more efficient than merely walking the halls.)

h. What problems the team typically brings to their attention and how they address them.

    i. How rapid turnover has been.

    j. How the candidates interact with their bosses. Are they manageable? Do they reflect the priorities of the department even if they don't find them important? How have their bosses gotten the best out of them? What do they disagree with their bosses about?

    k. If a politically charged environment agrees with the candidates and how they manage office politics.

    l. Ask them to outline their professional goals.

    m. Ultimately, with the help of some probing, you should be able to determine if the candidate will be able to do the job. This does not mean you will have a handle on whether this will become the final candidate.

18. How to probe – Following up on any of these questions is the real art of interviewing. Here is how to get the interviewee to explain more than planned.

    a. Encouragement – This can be done as simply as "Really? Tell me more."

    b. Mirroring – e.g., "So meeting this deadline was difficult?"

c. Probing – e.g., "Why do you think this occurred?"

d. Silence – If you have entered a useful area, shut up and listen. Maybe nod to keep the candidate talking. This is probably the most powerful probing tool. If candidates are uncomfortable with a little silence, what does this say about their confidence?

e. If the candidate starts to ramble, gently interrupt with a guiding question. Likewise, if the candidate over explains, gentle guidance is an essential tool in moving to more productive territory. If you are the hiring manager, it is a good idea to establish this authority up front.

f. If the candidate fails to answer the question, either by dissembling or misunderstanding, ask again. Getting the answer is important, especially if the candidate is trying to duck the question.

19. In evaluating the candidate's responses, you are looking for:

a. Clear definition of the problem or situation

b. Description of the candidate's actions

c. The outcome

iv. AREAS TO AVOID: Laws have been enacted to prevent discrimination in hiring. You must refrain from asking questions in the interview process that could be understood to be evaluating candidates in a variety of areas. Areas you must steer clear of:

1. National origin or birthplace

2. Religion

3. Age. Discrimination on the basis of age is prohibited by the Age Discrimination Act of 1975. Anyone over forty is protected.

4. Marital status or sexual preference

5. Disabilities. The Americans with Disabilities Act seeks to prevent discrimination on the basis of physical or emotional impairment. It does not, however, require you to hire people who cannot perform the essential functions of the job. Consult an attorney if faced with real questions, since the law is complex and confusing.

E. ATTIRE AND PERSONAL PRESENTATION: Depending on the nature of the job, personal comportment is more or less important. It is more important for a sales executive to make a strong personal impression than for an accountant. Your own attitudes play a role in this too. These days, determining the dress code is difficult for a candidate. Casual Fridays have expanded to the entire week. The candidate should be dressed appropriately; that is the only rule. A candidate should be clever enough to figure out how to look respectable. Attire is an important form of communication. Ideally, a candidate should be at least as dressed up as the interviewer.

F. **Humor:** Hiring managers almost always say they want the person they hire to possess a sense of humor. A sense of humor can be an important part of your corporate culture and may be valuable in building relationships within the company. Assessing this, however, can be difficult in an interview. This isn't really the right setting for a lot of humorous exchanges. In fact, too many wisecracks from the candidate could be a bad sign. If you are really interested in exploring the candidate's sense of humor, start the ball rolling yourself. Offer a humorous observation, if you are up to it, to see if the person responds in kind. Let him/her know that such things are acceptable during the conversation.

G. **Length of an interview:** It is difficult to conduct a thorough interview in less than fifty minutes. This is the minimum. Many interviewers, including experienced executive recruiters, require longer. To keep an interview short, be efficient:

   i. Be cordial but stay on track.

   ii. Be prepared to interrupt if the candidate gasses on.

   iii. Offer follow-up questions to guide the conversation, allowing you to get the most out of it.

   iv. Have a mental or written outline of what you want to accomplish.

    v. After achieving your goals, thank candidates for their time, establish next steps, and walk them to their next destination.

H. Taking notes: Definitely take notes, usually elaborate ones. If you interview frequently, you should make a note describing the person's appearance, not as a judgment but to remind you later which candidate was which.

I. Extricating yourself: It has happened to all of us: despite careful prescreening, it becomes obvious during the interview that the candidate is inappropriate for the job. Having asked the person in for an interview, you need to be polite but not spend a full hour going through the motions. The minimum time to spend, without being rude, is probably fifteen minutes. At that point simply thank the candidate for his/her time and close the interview. This can involve:

    i. Let the candidate know he/she will be hearing from you about next steps. In this case, avoid selling the position too hard.

    ii. Muster your courage and let the candidate know there are other candidates with stronger credentials. Don't try this if you are not the ultimate decision maker, in case the decision maker disagrees.

J. Selling: Once you have established that you are in the presence of a desirable candidate, then it's time to sell. It is also easier to sell once you know something about the interviewee and can tailor your pitch to the person's needs and experiences. Waiting to the end also saves you time. Don't spend time selling if the candidate isn't promising.

K. QUESTIONS: Always invite candidates to ask questions, usually toward the end of the meeting. Some hiring managers judge candidates on the quality of their questions. This can be a mistake, especially if you are the last interview of the day or if the candidate is well acquainted with your company or the job. All their questions may have been answered already. On the other hand, an insightful question can indicate a probing mind. Q&A is a good time to go into more detail about your goals for the position, details you perhaps didn't want to divulge at the beginning of the interview to prevent candidates from tailoring their comments.

L. CLOSING: Thank the candidate for coming. It has taken a lot of time for him/her to come to see you. Be warm. Make sure the hand-off happens smoothly so that the candidate slides seamlessly into whatever happens to be next on the schedule.

XX. Post-interview Assessment

a. NARROW THE FIELD: If you have evaluated a panel of four candidates in the first round, your goal is to narrow the field to two, a first and second choice.

b. CRITERIA FOR EVALUATION:

   i. Technical skills – This should be the easy part. Looking at the candidate's prior jobs will be a key indicator. Determine if the candidate has the ability and qualifications to perform the job. Since you are looking to winnow the slate of candidates in the first round of interviews, identifying a candidate who is not qualified helps to move this process along.

   ii. Cultural fit – This is much tougher. Sometimes more than one meeting is needed to unwrap this question. You are looking for people who will flourish in your organization. Even though it is important to make a preliminary assessment of fit in this round, the second and third interviews will focus on this in greater depth.

   iii. There are three kinds of interviews: good, bad, and in-between. The good and bad ones are easy and can be handled quickly, although you may want to spend a bit more time with the really good ones to sell the job. The in-between interviews are the most difficult and require the most time.

c. **FEEDBACK FROM THE INTERVIEWERS:** Collect feedback from everyone on your team who has interviewed the candidate. Talk with each one about what they liked and did not like and whether they could envision the candidate as a productive member of the team. Collect comments right away, but take others' opinions with a grain of salt. Their agendas may not coincide with yours. As the hiring manager, the hiring decision is up to you. The others on the panel are for advice and, unless it is your boss who has a strong reaction, should not be allowed veto power. Don't forget to collect feedback from the receptionist. Were the candidates pleasant, polite? Write all this down and make sure it is in a file that you can access readily.

d. **DECISION FACTORS:** When to accept a candidate and when to keep looking. Judge candidates according to the spec, the criteria you have determined up front that is necessary for success. Keep a list of the "must haves" at hand when reviewing candidates and make certain they meet the criteria. In this first round, your goal is to make sure the candidates can do the job, that they have sufficient technical skills. However, you also need to judge candidates according to the fit, the culture, the chemistry. Find someone you want to be around because you will be spending a lot of time with this person. One senior executive calls this the airplane test! He makes hiring decisions based on whether he would want to be on a cross-country airplane ride with this person.

e. **AVOID THE PERFECTION TRAP:** If you ask probing questions, you are likely to discover shortcomings. Avoid the temptation to jettison a candidate once you discover a flaw. No one is perfect. Remember, you are looking for someone who can be successful in a specific job and in your company. There is no honor in maintaining unreasonably high standards.

f. **THE IMPORTANCE OF MULTIPLE INTERVIEWS:** Clients often mistakenly believe they should be able to spot talent in the course of the initial interview. Very few have this sort of eye. In fact, a couple of follow-up conversations may be essential. This may prolong the process, but you will probably want to have several face-to-face meetings with a desirable candidate before making the hire. It is very important for you, the hiring manager, to find someone with whom you have a strong rapport. Go ahead, have several meetings in different environments to get a feel for what it would be like to work with this person. This is much more important than arranging for candidates to meet a wide variety of other semi-relevant executives.

g. **POST-INTERVIEW COURTESY:**

   i. Communication from the candidates: Many candidates send thank you letters after the interview (both electronic and handwritten are appropriate). Most do, some don't; probably 60/40 percent. Clients sometimes judge candidates on whether they send a note, and some even try to judge the quality of the note. The thank you note represents a miniscule bit of information about the candidate, not enough to make a judgment about his/her manners or ability to build relationships. Resist the temptation to make too much of a thank you note.

ii. Communication to the candidates:

1. Commmunicate promptly with every candidate. This is important. Even the most unappealing ones deserve letters or e-mails thanking them for their interest and time and assuring them that their information will be kept on file for future opportunities. Nothing creates more ill will than a lack of follow-up. Nearly every executive can tell a story of being courted by a company and then dropped without a word of explanation or follow-up. The person always remembers which company and which recruiters were thoughtless and unprofessional. Don't be on that list. Insist on thorough and prompt follow-up. Since your recruiters are representing you, make sure that they uphold the same high standard. Many don't!

2. An e-mail or even a call to a particularly desirable candidate to express your interest sends a powerful message. Don't underestimate its importance in convincing a candidate that your company is the right one. Just as you are assessing fit, so is the candidate. By extending yourself via a note or particularly through a call, you vastly increase your stature and desirability in the mind of the candidate.

h. **MOMENTUM:** At most there should be a couple of weeks between rounds of interviews. During that time someone (the hiring manager, HR, or the search firm) should be assigned to communicate regularly to "keep the candidates warm." It is extremely difficult for candidates to retain a high level of excitement about an opportunity if there are months in between rounds of interviews. They will withdraw for other jobs or perhaps just lose interest. If this is an important hire, make sure to keep the process rolling. Even though you are busy, long delays can cause the search to fail.

XXI. **The Second Interview**

a. By this point you should have winnowed the pool of candidates from approximately four to perhaps two. This is the serious courtship phase, and interviewers should be prepared to sell. Questions should focus more on "fit" issues, since competence and technical skills will have been stressed in the first round.

b. THE "OFF CAMPUS" INTERVIEW: In the second round you, the hiring manager, should interview the candidates again. These should be longer, less structured meetings, preferably away from the office and possibly over a meal. This allows you to get to know the candidates in a more comfortable setting. It can be very revealing, as you spend time away from a rigid office setting. Conversations often veer into personal subjects. Hard-line interview questions should be shelved during a meal. Focus instead on finding out the candidates' goals and motivations, what they are proudest of. It becomes easier to observe their personal confidence, thinking style, and personality in this setting when there is less pressure to be "on." Observe the way the candidates treat others and how decisive they are in ordering. Make sure to find a comfortable place where you can talk, and let the candidates do most of the talking.

c. OTHER INTERVIEWERS: Even though you have probably taken the candidates out for a meal, the rest of the second-round interviews should be done at the office. In the second round, include your boss and other important executives. There will be pressure to include a cast of thousands. Resist. You may be tempted to include members of your team who will be peers of the successful candidate. Peers come to the interview with their own agendas, some of which will conflict with yours. You certainly do not want to allow the successful candidate's future peers to sit in judgment. Keep the interview panel small to avoid losing control of the process. To maintain control of the process, prepare some notes on the candidates for the other interviewers, including any concerns and issues you would like them to explore. While you need to take your boss's concerns seriously, feel free to override the reactions of other interviewers if they are too critical. No candidate will please everyone.

d. **GOALS:** In the second round, you will attempt to identify an acceptable first and second choice. If neither of your candidates survives this round, you will have to start the process all over again. If the first interview focused on "must have" skills and eliminating the least qualified, this round requires more subtlety. You should focus on:

   i. Fit: Determine who shares the key characteristics necessary to succeed within your corporate culture, which you carefully outlined before you starting interviewing. Sample questions:

   1. "Tell me about your favorite employer and why."

   2. "What have you heard about our company?"

ii. Motivation: Identify what motivates the candidates. How driven they are, how willing to do the unpleasant aspects of the job. You may be able to get at some of this by questions like:

1. "What traits have contributed most to your success so far?"

2. "How do you rate your career so far and what do you plan to do to improve?"

3. "What goals have you set for yourself, either short or long term?"

4. "What have you done to improve your performance?"

iii. Decisiveness and leadership: Assess these characteristics by using a behavioral approach, asking about past successes and failures.

iv. Energy and work ethic: You will never get a candid response by asking directly. Better to ask questions that get at this indirectly:

1. "Describe a typical day."

2. "Describe your role and contributions in a recent project you worked on."

3. "Tell me about a project that required additional effort."

4. "How do you organize your time?"

v. Composure:

1. "Tell me about an emergency and how you reorganized responsibilities to get things done."

2. "What would you do...(in a crisis)?" (This utilizes situational rather than behavioral questioning.)

3. "Tell me about a time when you had more to do than you possibly could handle."

e. NO BACKUP CANDIDATE: At this point it can be a little scary if you have a lead candidate but no acceptable back-up. If you do have one, keep that person warm by communicating regularly. If you don't, make sure your recruiters are scouring the marketplace to find one. Try to ensure that your back-up candidate is strong enough to get an offer just in case your lead candidate flames out.

XXII. **The Third Interview**

During the third and final set of interviews you should achieve the following goals: confirm your judgment about the final candidate; choose between the two front runners if you are in a quandary; cover political bases, such as a meeting with the CEO, if required; and court the finalist candidate. More specifically, you should:

a. ANSWER QUESTIONS: The hiring manager must play the lead role, making sure that the finalists' questions are answered and that they understand all the benefits and challenges of the job. Explain how they will fit into your team and make sure they understand the potential for upward mobility.

b. COMMUNICATE: Either you or your recruiter should be talking frequently with the candidate. At this point it can be valuable to "pre-close", asking the candidate if he/she really wants this job and would accept an offer. This is not the time to negotiate the terms of the offer, only to ensure the candidate is interested. As the hiring manager, you or your recruiter should be expressing loads of enthusiasm to the candidate, but falling short of making or promising an offer.

c. PREPARE THE INTERVIEWERS: By this point you have invested a great deal of time in the process. It would be a shame if it went off the rails due to a lack of preparation. Make sure all the "higher ups" understand the key elements of the job and how you feel about the candidate(s). Make sure they review resumes and other relevant materials in advance. Outline your goals clearly, especially if any members of this final interview panel tend to be mavericks.

d. HAVE AN ALTERNATIVE PLAN: Allow new candidates to be submitted late in the process. It is not unheard of for a new candidate to emerge at the eleventh hour who blows away the rest of the contenders. Let your recruiters know that you expect them to keep looking even though a good group is under consideration.

e. DEAL WITH THE BACKUP CANDIDATE: This is always awkward. In an ideal world, once you conclude the second round of interviews, you will have a first and second choice, both of whom are acceptable. At some point you will have to focus on the primary candidate while keeping the second choice warm. This means that you or the executive recruiter must communicate regularly with the backup candidate to say that he or she is still under consideration. This is a tricky process because sometimes it takes a few weeks to negotiate with the finalist candidate, check references, and close the deal. If the last stage of the search drags on, there is a danger that the backup candidate will feel you have been dealing in bad faith. There is little that can be done about this, short of keeping the process moving quickly and communicating regularly with the backup candidate. After all, you don't want to sign off your backup candidate before successfully hiring your top choice.

XXIII. **Investigate the Finalist Candidate**

There are various ways of assessing whether your finalist candidate is what he or she appears to be. Nothing is foolproof, but using these steps provides some assurance against being bamboozled. Typically these steps are taken once you have identified a single finalist you want to hire, but before an offer is extended. An executive recruiter, if you are using one, will likely take care of these issues.

a. REFERENCE CHECKS: References are essential, but checking them has become more difficult recently because former employers are increasingly cautious about the potential legal liability of a negative reference. Employees at some companies have been instructed only to confirm that the employee worked at the company; nothing qualitative. It is tempting but not legal for you to contact others who are not on the list of approved references provided by the candidate. This makes the quality of references suspect because almost anyone can find at least a few fans. This restrictive environment has made the reference check less important and a less useful way to validate your choice of a successful candidate. Despite the difficulties, it is possible and valuable to get candid, thorough references. They will be helpful, although perhaps not as much as they would have been in yesterday's less restrictive environment. Here is what to expect:

i. Six references, more or less, from business
    colleagues who have had the opportunity
    to work closely with the candidate. The best
    approach is to contact references who are "up,
    down, and across," or bosses, subordinates, and
    peers. The candidate will be prepared to supply
    names, contact information, and the nature of the
    relationship. Insist on professional, not personal
    references.

ii. References should reveal the candidate's level
    of skills, performance, and success. Typically the
    executive recruiter will conduct references. If you
    haven't hired a recruiter, HR will likely handle it. In
    either case you should receive a written or, at the
    very least, a verbal descriptions of the references.
    Most important are suggestions of how best to
    manage and get the best performance from the
    candidate.

iii. You, as the hiring manager, may want to contact
     one or several references yourself, probably
     a former boss. This allows you to solicit tips on
     how to manage the candidate and get the best
     performance possible. This also shows your
     commitment to the hiring process and to bringing
     on the best possible talent. This is not at all
     mandatory.

iv. Lawyers may tell you not to leave written
    references in your files to prevent the possibility
    of future liability. In the real world, this almost
    never becomes a problem.

v. Below is a list of questions you can use in conducting a reference. Remember that open-ended questions are best:

1. Identify the relationship between the reference and the candidate—how long and how well they have known the candidate? Was this person a boss, peer or subordinate of the candidate? How long since they worked with the candidate?

2. Begin with an open ended question: "Tell me about the candidate." This often leads to follow-up probes.

3. Briefly describe the job. Ask if it sounds like a good fit for the candidate.

4. On a scale of one to ten, how would you rate the candidate's performance? Keep in mind that no one rates anyone a ten. Then follow up with, "What could/should the candidate have done to improve that ranking to a ten?" This gets the reference talking about a person's shortcomings, which is always difficult to get a reference to do.

5. Was the candidate successful in your organization? This also elicits rich responses.

6. Why did the candidate leave your company? Could he/she have stayed if he/she wanted?

7. What advice would you give to the candidate's new boss?

8. How did the candidate fit in with coworkers in the culture of your organization?

9. Is there a particular culture that the candidate should strive to be in or to avoid?

10. What are the candidate's strengths and weaknesses?

11. Is there anything I'm missing and should be asking?

12. Were there performance issues that would be helpful to know about?

13. Describe the candidate's management/leadership style? Was he/she well regarded by his/her team?

14. Is the candidate more of an implementer or initiator of strategy?

15. What were the candidate's key accomplishments? What was he/she known for?

16. What areas of development should the candidate work on?

17. How well did the candidate deal with:

    i. Senior management

    ii. Stressful situations

        iii. Office politics

        iv. Difficult people

        v. His/her team

   18. Would you work with this person again? Why? If you get a qualified response such as "under the right circumstances" find out what those circumstances are. This can be revealing.

b. **BACKGROUND CHECKS:** These are performed by a third party, not by the search firm, although the search firm will likely be able to make recommendations. You will also need the candidate's written agreement to perform them. There are reputable firms that will investigate credit and criminal records, employment verification, and substance abuse issues.

c. **ONLINE ASSESSMENTS:** These are gaining in popularity but unlikely to be accurate predictors of success. Frankly, I am not a fan. These tests attempt to interpret a candidate's ability and such gauges as "fit" or "leadership." They are usually provided by third parties and should not be viewed as factual or essential hurdles before an offer. They merely supplement your judgment. Assessments cannot replace the other steps described in this book. Hiring managers who lack the courage of their convictions often view these assessments as highly reliable and dump candidates who score poorly. Big mistake. These tests do not possess that level of predictive power.

d. **DEGREE CHECKS:** Checking whether the candidate actually possesses the university degrees claimed on the resume is one of the easiest ways to determine whether the candidate is truthful. The university or a service they have hired will provide this information, sometimes for a small fee. Always check degrees. False claims happen infrequently, but when you catch someone in a lie, this should end their candidacy.

e. CHECKING COMPENSATION: Most employers and executive recruiters trust the candidate to provide accurate information on their current and past compensation. If it seems out of line or if you are natively suspicious, feel free to ask for W-2 forms to substantiate this information. However, it is highly unusual for a company to make this request. Candidates may be offended.

f. ONGOING COMMUNICATIONS: The process described above takes time, maybe a week. Since this is a stressful time for the candidate who is waiting for an offer, why not give him/her a call. Without making promises, since the offer hasn't been made and can still go off the rails, reassure the candidate and express enthusiasm.

XXIV. **Closing**

a. MAKING THE CHOICE: Choosing the finalist candidate can be agonizing. In evaluating candidates, clients often make the mistake of focusing exclusively on the technical requirements. Sometimes the person with all the skills is not the right choice. Fit, leadership, and long-term talent potential trump specific skills. The candidate with more potential will be more successful than the one who meets all the specs.

b. ENSURING INTEREST: Pursue your chosen candidate with regular attention, communication, and enthusiasm. You, the hiring manager, should be involved in these efforts. This strategy is called "surround and hound." Whatever you call it, expressing interest in the finalist will improve your chances of closing successfully. This is important!

c. MONEY:

    i. Compensation is rarely the primary reason someone accepts a job, but the numbers must work or the transaction will not be concluded successfully.

    ii. Typically, if a candidate is happily employed, an offer must be AT LEAST 15 percent more than that person's current compensation and perhaps as much as 30 percent or more for the person to accept. If the candidate is unemployed, you may be able to get away with an offer at parity with that person's last job.

iii. By this time you should have an understanding of the candidate's current or most recent compensation. You should also be able to make a good estimate of what it will take to attract the lead candidate. If you don't, have an open conversation with the candidate right away.

iv. Much of your decision about the offer is made at the outset of the search. Especially in larger corporations, you will be limited to a narrow range according to the level of the job. Not much you can do about that.

v. Occasionally the hiring manager will have fallen in love with a more senior candidate who requires compensation that exceeds your expectations. Don't be afraid to go do battle with top management to get the extra money.

vi. A lowball offer, less than the candidate is earning or earned at his/her most recent job, is usually a bad idea. First, the candidate will likely refuse and may even cut off further negotiations because he/she concludes you have been negotiating in bad faith. Even if the candidate must accept the lowball offer, there are likely to be hard feelings that will lead the candidate to leave at the first opportunity. You may think you are a tough negotiator, but that person probably won't stick around for long.

vii. If you are courting a candidate who exceeds your comp parameters, let the candidate know up front, early in the search. In the previous section, you were advised not to extend a lowball offer. This is particularly true if you haven't discussed it in advance with the candidate. You may get away with it, however, if you have been forthright from the beginning about the limits of your ability to pay. This is dangerous territory.

d. PREPARING THE OFFER: Every company will have its own procedures for preparing and approving the offer. The legal department is always consulted. Most of the effort goes into establishing the compensation to be offered, which usually includes the base salary, a targeted bonus, and a long-term incentive and/or equity program. There is usually a bit of gamesmanship involved. Companies often extend the initial offer, leaving a modest amount in reserve in case the candidate negotiates. Most candidates are aware of this and try to negotiate for more once the offer has been extended. The difference between the initial offer and the final offer is rarely significant.

e. MOTIVATION: In extending an offer, it is important to understand what candidates are looking for in a new job. The order of importance of these criteria, which rarely changes, is:

  i. professional challenge and opportunity

  ii. a good fit with the organization

      iii. compensation, which is rarely the top motivator, but the number has to work or the candidate will reject the offer

f. **NEGOTIATING THE DEAL:** It is usually best to allow the executive recruiter to extend the offer and negotiate the deal. If the negotiations become testy, this reduces the likelihood of hard feelings. If you insist on extending the offer, consider allowing the recruiter or HR to "test drive" the numbers with the candidate to make sure you are headed for an acceptance. Do not expect an acceptance on the spot. Candidates will usually want to see an offer letter and to think about it for couple of days before accepting. Most candidates will push back, asking for more money. It is helpful to have a little in reserve to close the deal. It also makes for good will with the candidate.

g. **OFFER LETTER:** An offer letter is essential to make sure that you and the candidate share a common understanding of the opportunity and its components. Make sure your legal department has reviewed it and that it contains all the particulars:

      i. Salary

      ii. Target bonus

      iii. Employment status, usually "at will"

      iv. Enthusiasm – convey how excited you are to have the candidate coming on board.

      v. Start date – not required on the letter but often included

vi. A place for the candidate to sign, indicating acceptance, along with instructions where to return it for your files

h. **COUNTEROFFER:** Getting all this distance with a candidate only to lose him or her to a counteroffer can be maddening, yet there is no foolproof way to prevent it. The executive recruiter, if there is one, should help prevent this by staying in close touch with the candidate, constantly taking his or her temperature. HR can perform this function as well. Toward the end of the courtship process, someone should discuss with the candidate whether there is likely to be a counteroffer. This person should ask how the candidate plans to react. This may allow you to find out if the candidate really has decided to leave. Occasionally a candidate will view the offer from you as a negotiating ploy to see if more money can be extorted from his/her current employer. This is unusual and is pretty sleazy. Companies may extend a counteroffer to fix a short-term problem, but many view the act of looking for a new job as a sign of disloyalty. The company can be annoyed that they have been held up by the candidate. Likewise, a counteroffer can be annoying to the candidate, who wonders why they have been paying so little if he/she is worth so much more. Accepting a counteroffer is often a bad idea. Those who accept the counteroffer are frequently removed from consideration for long-term growth opportunities. A smart, ethical, decisive candidate firmly decides to leave his/her current employer and accept the new offer before going in to resign.

i. **COMPETING OFFERS:** If candidates are unemployed, they will be pursuing other opportunities, and you will need to ask periodically if they are getting close to another acceptable offer. Your recruiter should actually be doing this. The recruiter should also be probing to see how your opportunity compares with others under consideration. The candidate should be open enough to rank the various opportunities under consideration, usually truthfully. If you are handling the courtship of the candidate yourself, make sure to cover this ground while keeping the candidate "warm." Timing is important. Don't lose a desirable candidate because you have failed to keep tabs on that person's other job prospects.

j. ACCEPTANCE: After the candidate accepts an offer, do something nice to indicate how excited you are. At the very least, call the person to express your enthusiasm. Calls from other members of your team will also mean a great deal. Some companies send a welcoming gift. Taking the candidate to lunch or dinner is also very welcoming.

k. START DATE:

   i. Whether or not the candidate is employed, interviewing for a new job is stressful. Whether the person realizes it or not, he/she needs a rest. Often the search has dragged on longer than expected, and you, the hiring manager, are eager to get the successful candidate on board. Nevertheless, allow the candidate to give a couple of weeks' notice and have another week to rest. Don't push the candidate to accept a premature start date. Not only is it stressful to look for a new job, starting a new job is stressful, too. When the successful candidate walks through your door, you will want him/her to be at his/her best.

ii. Some candidates, being either ready to go or gluttons for punishment, will decline the offer of a week's rest. I think this is a mistake.

iii. On the other hand, don't allow the candidate to remain at the current job for longer than a few weeks. Some candidates try to insist, under the guise of "not wanting to burn bridges". This sort of misplaced loyalty usually stems from a candidate's guilt about leaving. A couple of weeks should be enough to wrap things up. Once they think about it, most employers don't want an employee around after resigning; it tends to hurt morale.

XXV. **Onboarding**

a. NEW HIRES SOMETIMES FAIL TO ADAPT TO A NEW JOB. Estimates of failure reach as high as 50 percent, although this sounds highly exaggerated. Any good recruiter guarantees to do the search again for free if the successful candidate leaves within the first year, but even so the time lost and potential disruption of a failed hire are enormous. Isn't it worthwhile, therefore, to ease the newly hired executive's transition to the new job?

b. THERE ARE A VARIETY OF ONBOARDING TECHNIQUES. Third-party career coaches are sometimes retained, which can be helpful but are expensive. Larger companies may have an orientation program. A good executive recruiter will typically stay in touch, but this is no substitute for an onboarding process. Perhaps the best way to ensure success is for you, the hiring manager, to pay particular attention during the first few months. Make sure the successful candidate settles in, builds relationships and learns how things get done. Assigning a mentor or buddy can useful. Even asking a few of your colleagues to take the new executive to lunch goes a long way in making the person feel at home.

XXVI. **What If Your Search Fails?**

a. EVEN THE BEST-RUN SEARCHES OCCASIONALLY FAIL TO RESULT IN A SUCCESSFUL HIRE. Sometimes no one qualified can be found. This can be your fault, if your standards are too high or if you aren't paying enough. Perhaps the recruiter hasn't looked hard enough or in the right places. If the market is hot, competition might be too stiff. Sometimes the recruitment drags on for months, putting strain on the existing staff. Sometimes you find someone desirable and just can't close. Sometimes you make a bad selection, and the damage to your team can be devastating. Here's how to avoid a failed search:

b. PAY ATTENTION TO THE SEARCH: If you have not seen qualified candidates within a month of searching, ask why. Then correct the problem. It could be from having the wrong people actually doing the searching, or it may relate to the parameters themselves (compensation, unnecessarily stringent standards).

c. TAKE PROACTIVE STEPS: Occasionally, despite your best efforts, the recruitment fails. If you have paid attention to the recruitment process, this will happen infrequently. What do you do if it still goes bust?

    i.   Reorganize your staff around the problem, which is usually only a Band-Aid, but perhaps you can split up the responsibilities among your existing team.

ii. Promote an internal candidate, although if there was a qualified one you probably would have promoted that person before going to all this trouble.

iii. Lower your standards or offer more compensation and continue the search.

iv. None of these solutions is desirable, reinforcing the importance of getting it done right the first time.

XXVII. **Advice from the Experts**

Below is a selection of hiring tips from prominent human resources executives:

Deb Josephs, Senior Vice President of Human Resources at eXelate

"Every interaction is a branding opportunity. From the moment you pitch a job, to the greeting at reception, to the offer letter or decline, remember that these communications are an extension of the company's brand. Recruiters we work with should embody this brand too and, even if the hire doesn't happen, ensure the candidate walks away feeling good about your company and perhaps be a source of other leads in the future."

Stuart Thompson, Vice President of Talent Management at Scripps Networks Interactive Inc.

"The best candidate is not just the most qualified and skilled candidate for the current need, they should also have the aspiration and potential to develop into an even bigger role for the company."

Fritz Maier, Senior Director of Global Recruitment at Revlon

"When I look at a resume I look for three things:

1. Does the person have a trajectory? In other words, have they been promoted over time? The reason is that high-potential employees tend to be promoted every couple of years over time. I believe that 'Winners' will continue to 'Win' if they are given the right environment to succeed. A steady increase in the scope of their responsibilities is important.

2. The second thing I look for is where they have worked and been successful. People succeed and are therefore effective in different types of workplace environments. For example, someone that may be a success at Proctor & Gamble may have difficulty in a less structured, highly cross-functional workplace.

3. Finally, I look for length of time at companies. Certainly, some fields change hands more than others, and people in their mid-careers change less than those just starting out, BUT the ability to stay with one employer for more than 3 years is important. If someone changes jobs every 12–24 months, to me that is a sign of someone that can't make it when the honeymoon period is over and the results are starting to show. Time tested, if you will."

Rodney W. Whitmore, Senior Vice President and Chief HR Officer at the Economist Group

"Talent acquisition is a subset of a broader talent strategy. Executive recruitment is only as effective as an organization's understanding of its own DNA. Without the alignment of senior executives regarding the technical and leadership competences that create value within their company, staffing success is likely random."

Kathleen Gioffre, Head of Talent Acquisition and Leadership Recruiting at Aetna

"I believe it is important to determine carefully what I should share as a firm selling to the candidate. While it is important for the candidate to sell themselves, they are evaluating us in the same manner we are evaluating them. I want them to walk away informed and educated to ensure they know as much as possible about us as an employer. It is a win-win if both parties know what they are getting. Oftentimes I like candidates to shadow or speak to someone who is performing the role they are being considered for. It's like 'the day in the life of.' A real true sense of what they would be getting into. I believe in sharing the good, bad, and the ugly—again so both parties know what they are getting.

"I always tell my team: 'treat every candidate as if they were your client.' No matter how wonderful or terrible the candidate may be, you want them to walk away having the most optimal experience. You never know who they know or if they will be a future client. It's about having ambassadors in the market. Everyone talks about their experience!"

Alan E. Gaynor, Senior Vice President of Human Resources at Frontier Communications

1. "It is critical to ask behavioral interview questions—How did you accomplish your objective? What obstacles did you have to overcome, what was the business result?

2. I also strongly recommend situational interview questions. Present a real-life problem and asked the candidate to solve it. LISTEN very closely to their thought process as to how they attempt to solve it.

3. Watch body language. Observe how people react to tough questions from their posture to their eye contact."

Arden Schneider, currently startup-focused HR leader, formerly Senior Vice President of Human Resources at Medidata Solutions

- "Talent Acquisition Strategy – 'It's all about the employer brand'

- The Interview Process – 'Tactical and practical'

"STRATEGY: The Employer Brand

"Strategically speaking, effective talent acquisition—attracting and hiring top talent—is all about employer branding. Organizations wisely spend a lot of time, creative brainpower, and money on corporate branding in order to set and convey high expectations for their products and/or services, thereby initiating a compelling customer experience. In the same way, every organization needs to define and communicate who they are, why top talent should want to join the team, and what employees can expect, thereby initiating a compelling candidate experience.

"Once you successfully establish and communicate your employer brand, 'recruitment' turns into 'attraction.' Think about how much easier it would be to hire top talent if you had a brand that attracts them, rather than forcing a team to go out and find and recruit them. Even if you are using an outside search firm, a recognizable, positive employer brand will streamline the process considerably.

"INTERVIEW PROCESS: Tactical and Practical

"As an HR professional, I have a list of some very basic best practices regarding the interview process that has been reinforced over the years through follow-up conversations with candidates and employees. These are purely tactical, and while they may seem obvious, so many employers/interviewers do not get it right. The common denominator here is respect for the candidate, and that respect must be instilled in the talent acquisition process from the top. From a strategic standpoint, the organization's culture needs to foster the notion that bringing in top talent is mission critical for the success of the organization. From a tactical standpoint, it's important to remember that candidates learn a lot about the culture of an organization by going through the interview process. The fundamentals:

- Be ready at the confirmed start time; just as you wouldn't want the candidate to make you wait, don't make the candidate wait.

- Offer water (and coffee or tea if available); the candidate is likely to be nervous.

- Bring your business card and hand it to the candidate before you start talking; a card will remind the candidate of your name and title/job function during the conversation and will provide your contact information for the candidate's thank-you note.

- Read the candidate's resume beforehand (and bring a copy with you); nothing is worse for a candidate than hearing 'I haven't looked at your resume; can you just tell me about yourself?'

- If you bring candidates in for a succession of meetings where they meet interviewers one after the other for hours at a stretch, offer lunch/food/beverages as well as breaks at appropriate intervals.

- After the interview, provide status updates to keep the candidate apprised and interested. If/when you decide that the candidate isn't a fit for the role, be honest and communicate that; this is especially important if the individual isn't right for the role at hand but might be perfect for a different role down the road. Even those you don't hire should be ambassadors for your employer brand."

Michael Mimnaugh, General Manager and Senior Vice President of Human Resources at ITOCHU International Inc.

"Although I ask the traditional questions pertaining to work history and qualifications, I like to focus on the individual in order to challenge their ability to think on their feet. For instance below in questions 1 thru 3, I am often more curious about the reply to the second or third part of the question versus the initial questions...the 'why' and/or 'what' did you learn from this experience? I will frequently ask multiple questions as a result of only one reply or statement on the applicants resume...all designed to focus the conversation on the candidate...and in a conversational manner.

1. What do you find are the most difficult decisions to make and why?

2. If you are confident that your boss is incorrect about something, how would you handle the situation?

3. Tell me about a significant business decision that you made which did not go according to your plan. Describe for me what went wrong and how you corrected the matter. What did you learn?

4. What is it about you that colleagues most criticize?

5. How would you describe the pace at which you work?"

Ed Spruck, Vice President of Human Resources at Revlon

1. "Measure everything. Metrics are fact-based, tangible evidence of how you're doing. They highlight where you're doing well and where you need to improve. Metrics can also be used as an objective tool to use with managers who are slow to turn around feedback or make time for interviews.

2. Leverage multiple interviewers to cover different aspects of the candidate that you want to understand better. This creates a coordinated approach and allows a deeper dive into areas you really want or need to understand (versus all the interviewers doing their own thing and covering much of the same information). It also creates a better candidate experience: 'The company really got to know me and gave me a chance to tell my story.'"

Kimberly Moffa, Chief Administrative Officer at A. Reddix & Associates (ARDX)

1. "Ask the question, 'What gets your goat?' This question for some reason generally gets a candidate to open up. I always get a real glimpse into their biases, frustrations, and how they process and deal with obstacles and challenges.

2. There are two types of leaders: those that build and those that maintain. Be sure you select the right one for the current and intermediate stage in the company lifecycle.

3. Hire talent that meets your needs today, but is more than adequately prepared and talented enough to have longevity into the not too distant future!

4. HIRE those with impeccable EQ: Emotional Intelligence and Executional Quotient."

Kenneth C. Rowe, Director of Human Resources at Scholastic Education

Scholastic Classroom & Community Group

"As much as it may be the candidate's responsibility to market herself, the interview experience is equally an opportunity for the prospective employer to entice the candidate—most particularly in the stage of weighing a final offer—to accept the interested organization as her new career 'home.' It's very compelling to a candidate to know she is highly regarded and wanted. To that end I often find it helpful to view the final stages as a form of courtship. That is, once much of the negotiating has been done and a final offer has been made, the personal touch of a token 'gift' such as a small bouquet of flowers, a fruit basket, or even a couple bottles of organic wine (if, for example, over conversation the candidate expressed interest in maintaining a healthy lifestyle), from the senior-most person within the organization leading the search—accompanied by a brief message conveying how hopeful the company is that the candidate consider joining the organization—can make all the difference in her decision-making process. The personal touch is especially compelling when it comes from an organization that's been utilizing third-party assistance in the form of executive search. It builds a special connection at a critical point. I learned this many years ago from a mentor CHRO, and it's just as relevant (and effective) today—especially with fierce competition for key talent."

Howard Marcus, Managing Director and Global Head of Professional and Leadership Development at BlackRock

"Our job as leaders is to make sure that our organizations are on a positive trajectory in terms of growth, effectiveness, and overall capability. I approach hiring with a pretty simple question—will this person add capability to our team; will he or she make us stronger, more effective, able to execute better, be more creative and responsive to our customers? In short, will this person challenge us, help us grow as a team and do more, and create more value and growth in the organization we serve?"

Andrea "Andi" Fenster, Senior Talent Acquisition Consultant at Under Armour

"Hire for core skills and passion…and not always in that order. Train for the rest."

Sharon Tunstall, Executive Coach and Leadership Development Consultant

"Some questions I often ask:

Describe to me a situation where you made a mistake. What did you learn from that experience? In retrospect would you have done things differently?

If I were to walk into your office/home/apt. what would I see? How would I describe the environment?

"Other thoughts:

When looking for talent I often look for people who have intense curiosity. If people are curious they generally like to learn, tend to be well rounded, often are more creative. I ask people about books they read (or in this digital age blogs they read, etc.) What kind of media do they frequent? It's easy for people to talk about skills and work experience, but you get a more complete picture by going into behavior that describes how a person thinks and what they like to do outside of work."

Marny Ridling, Director of Recruitment at Turner Broadcasting

"The days of post and wait (or pray) are gone. Recruiting has become an art of long-distance relationship management. Candidates are found in social media forums or through networking infiltration and espionage. It's no longer looking under every rock but digging beneath and around them. As you court your candidates through these platforms, you gain new candidates to court until you have opportunities to present. You hope that your long-distance relationship has the strength to get them to nibble, and if not, you keep courting until they do."

Sharon Jautz, Director of Talent Acquisition at Sandow Media

"Tell me about a time when being honest didn't pay off for you.

Tell me about a time you made a big mistake. How did you handle it? Did you tell your boss?

Talk to me about something you are passionate about.

What is the riskiest thing you have ever done?

How do you implement/execute on an idea you disagree with?"

Michael Bruno, Senior Vice President of Human Resources for Search at IAC

"As a hiring leader, you should always do a deep dive into a candidate's resume searching for the following:

- What did they actually accomplish in each position…dig under the covers.

- How did they accomplish the results…individual or team…the process used to get the actual results?

- Why was this accomplishment important to the overall success of the company? Did it contribute to the growth of the company?

- When was the accomplishment completed…timeline factor…do they work with a sense of urgency?

- You want to determine their critical thinking skills, process management, and impact for the organization."

Anonymous, Executive Vice President of Human Resources for a major media company

"I still follow the advice of what I was taught when I first started interviewing thirty-plus years ago. It has served me well whether I was interviewing a C-suite candidate or a secretary.

"Open the conversation by making small talk. It forces the candidate to breathe, which helps him/her relax.

"Make sure the person leaves you feeling no worse, and hopefully better, for having spoken to you. It says a lot to the candidate about your company and you!"

Regina Angeles, Senior Partner and Director at Mindshare, Talent Acquisition North America

"My favorite reference question: What type of person would you partner with this candidate to maximize their strengths?

"The Rule of 150: According to Malcolm Gladwell, it takes 150 people talking about something to create a tipping point, and it's the same benchmark for a search. So every time I conduct a search, I target a minimum of 150 contacts to create the buzz around the role and get a referral network activated. Sometimes it happens faster depending on the role, but it's a very helpful guideline especially when you are feeling stuck."

Chris Powell, CEO of BlackbookHR

"Don't Fall in Love Too Quickly.

"Over the years, I have kissed a lot of frogs in my quest to recruit top talent. One key lesson that I have learned through experience is don't fall in love with top talent too quickly.

"Love at first sight can be real, but in many cases the feeling is not deeper than a paper cut. What may appear to be love was usually some strong positive bias I had toward a talent's previous work or educational experience, their intellect, their career mobility, their ability to engage me, and last but not least their presence. You know they looked or sounded the part.

"The key to finding Mr. or Ms. Right is to spend time getting to know and understand the dimensions of the candidate. As attractive as the wrapper may be, I always make sure to evaluate three things: skill set, mind-set, and experience. This helps me form a multidimensional perspective of the candidate. And although it's been useful for me, it's not perfect. As it has been said before, slow to hire quick to fire."

Christine Ellis Roggenbusch, Human Resources Director at Facebook

- "I like to be personally involved in the negotiation of an executive's package. I find this the most meaningful interaction pre-hire because you really get a sense for what the person cares about and how they negotiate and communicate. If I don't feel like I can have an honest dialogue with the person at this stage, then I have to wonder what kind of relationship we will have once they are on board.

125

- Don't assume that past successes guarantee future success. There's a lot of randomness and good and bad luck in business, and an exec shouldn't get credit for being in the right place, with the right people, at the right time. Show me your thought process, tell me how you accomplished the things you accomplished, give proper credit to those who helped you, and I will feel more confident you can handle the complexities that will come our way.

- I want to hear about an exec's failures. The real ones. The ones that made them think they were done, that were embarrassing and painful, and that are still difficult to talk about. This will tell me how they learn, and it tells me how honest they are willing to be. Transparency in an exec is so critical to being able to develop and lead a team."

Betty Panarella, Senior Vice President of Human Resources at Asset International

"One of the common mistakes senior management makes is to try to hire heads of companies, thinking that they will bring the secret of success with them. They don't. Hire the second or third in command. They do all the real work and know the product best. The chairman depends on them for their guidance. I can list several times when we brought in heads of successful companies to head up one of our businesses, and it was a waste of time and money, big money as you can imagine."

William Kelley, Director of Talent at Ford Foundation

"Human resources practitioners need to keep in mind that as we are evaluating candidates, they are also evaluating us."

Jeriann Kolton, Principal at JAK Insights

"Know your company and culture and be completely honest in coming up with the job description and desired traits. Spend time on the job profile and get other stakeholders' input and buy-in. Once you're all clear in what you're looking for, it will be easier to have a meaningful conversation about the right candidate. And you'll be setting up your new employee for effective onboarding since the team is aligned around the role and the person filling that role.

"To do the job profile, you'll need to think long and hard about where the company and department are headed in the next few years. Is innovation critical? Or is it inspiring and motivating a team? Or is it process improvement? Then tailor questions to that.

"I've seen the greatest leaders fall in the trap of thinking they need to hire a type of leader that isn't really a right fit for their company. For example, everyone likes to say innovation is critical, but if you hire someone who loves change, there may be culture clash with your company, which, when you really think about it, wants a methodical approach to process improvement, not a radical innovation.

"If you want someone with great people management skills, look for someone who has proven themselves—i.e., had long-term employees who've been promoted. Ask about those specifics, not just their 'management philosophy,' which anyone can answer in a way that sounds appealing in an interview.

"So:

1) Be clear with what you want. Make sure it is specific and targeted, but not merely a laundry list of adjectives.

2) Get buy-in to the job profile.

3) Ask specific, behavioral questions to ascertain those skills."

Peter Phelan, Senior Vice President of Human Resources at Media Math

"Trust your instincts! If even the faintest alarm bell is ringing about any aspect of a candidate's fit for the company culture and/or role—probe with behavioral interview questions / unofficial reference checks until your concern is addressed one way or another.

"Before hiring a senior executive as a change agent, have them prepare a 180-day business plan and use it as a prop for the interviews—including the meetings with those who'll report into the hire. If the positive change feels like it's already happening before you even extend the offer, you're likely onto a good thing. If not, do not hire that individual.

"Directly address with the candidate how they would respond to a counteroffer from their current job before you extend the offer."

Susan Gunn, SVP Global Talent at Aramark

"Never underestimate the power of the candidate experience. No matter how successful a company or team may be, your responsibility is not only to assess the candidate for their potential fit and capabilities, but also to engage them to want YOU. Top talent have choices. Make sure you become their number one."

Brian Harmsen, Founder and CEO of Designworks Talent LLC

"I'm always screening candidates for problem-solving skills. Employees with strong problem-solving ability consistently outperform their peers regardless of industry or function."

Jeanette M. Ercila, Global Talent Acquisitions Leader at LinkedIn

- "Ensure you have a bar raiser in the interview process. This person should be responsible for elevating the talent brought into the organization. Never settle.

- Hire someone that's about two-thirds right for the job and give them about one-third of the way to grow. This will ensure they can have a path on the team and in the company. That's a two-way hire."

Sandy Lau, Human Resources at Comcast Corporation

"My main advice to any hiring manager, or recruiter, for that matter, is to interview with the intent of disqualifying the candidate. In other words, hiring managers should find all the reasons why a candidate is not suitable.

"I approach most of my interviews that way, and at the end of the ones where I absolutely cannot find reasons to not hire, that tells me that we have a winner."

Marie Mann, Senior Vice President of Human Resources at Neopost USA

"It is important to follow up with every candidate. Keep them apprised of their status along the way and always close the loop regardless of the outcome of the search. Candidates want to know where they stand—and it will leave them with a favorable impression of the search firm and the client company if there is good communication."

Jim Young, Executive Vice President and Chief Human Resources Officer at Collective

"Do your own reference checks. You'll get quite a lot of insight into your potential hire. You may learn something that better informs your hiring decision. Or you may find a particular strength or area of development that may influence how you get your new employee off to a good start.

"Be wary of long yeses. If a candidate is taking too long to accept, chances are they aren't the best hire. Have a backup plan ready."

Linda Tepedino, Vice President of Human Resources at Consumer Reports

"As with a hire at any level, know what you need and keep it simple. That doesn't mean a job description for a leadership position shouldn't be exciting or inspirational. However, too much time is often spent on perfecting the description and hiring goals that turn out to be unrealistic for one person. It can become a setup for either a failed search or impossible expectations—resulting in a failed hire. When you are preparing the job specs think about the reason for the opening:

What is the core need? What key role must be filled? How must this person complement the rest of the executive team? What is the right cultural fit? What are the deal breakers? Remember, no one person can be a savior. They are joining a team. Every member must play a role on the team and support each other. One person cannot close the organization's entire talent gap or solve all its problems.

"Acquiring talent is similar to acquiring a business. One of the lessons I learned from doing a lot of due diligence for company acquisitions is that many of them fail because of a poor cultural fit. Not only does the business model need to work, the culture must be a fit. In acquiring talent, keep the core values of your organization in mind. If the candidate does not share them, there is a strong chance they will become a 'bad hire.'"

Suki Parsons, HR Consultant at JWT

"Go ahead and see the out of the box candidate. Hiring Managers say they want to, but then they never do and they hire the ones from the obvious places. Even if you don't hire the out of the box candidate, the interview will provide perspective about trends in the marketplace.

When you interview senior level candidates, keep in mind this can be a networking opportunity for you. You never know when the shoe might be on the other foot."

NJ Pesci, Executive Vice President of Human Resources at Scripps Networks Interactive:

In recruiting senior executives, you have your spec, the resumes of candidates, and the reality of what the job entails.

Always keep in mind that there are huge differences be-tween them. It is difficult but essential to line up the reality, particularly between what the candidate says on the resume and what the successful candidate will actually encounter in the job. Solving this dilemma requires honesty from the em-ployer about what the job really is and not just what you want it to be. It also requires deep probing of the candidate's background, going well beyond the resume.

An Invitation:

There is an ever-so-slight chance that all of your questions about handling the recruiting process have not been addressed. If so, please feel free to e-mail Rick Linde at rick@chemistryexecutivesearch.com.